THE
NATURE
DIRECTORY

SUSAN D. LANIER-GRAHAM

THE
NATURE
DIRECTORY

A Guide to
Environmental Organizations

· WALKER AND COMPANY ·
New York

This book is dedicated to my son, Patrick. I hope, in some small way, Patrick, that this book makes a contribution to your future. I grew up loving the smell of fresh air and the beauty of the world around me. I hope the same for you and your generation.

This book is also for my husband, Bill. Thanks, Bill, for believing in me and for dreaming with me. I know I made the right choice!

I love you both.

First published in the United States of America in 1991 by Walker Publishing Company, Inc.

Published simultaneously in Canada by Thomas Allen & Son Canada, Limited, Markham, Ontario

Library of Congress Cataloging-in-Publication Data
Lanier-Graham, Susan D.
    The nature directory / Susan D. Lanier-Graham.
      p.   cm.
    Includes bibliographical references and index.
    ISBN 0-8027-1151-0. —ISBN 0-8027-7348-6 (pbk.)
    1. Environmental protection—Societies, etc.—Directories.
2. Nature conservation—Societies, etc.—Directories. I. Title.
TD169.L36   1991
363.7'0025'7—dc20   91-6649
                                 CIP

Text Design by Susan Phillips

Printed in the United States of America

2 4 6 8 10 9 7 5 3 1

Contents

Acknowledgments

So many people have helped me, both directly and indirectly, in making this book a reality. My editor at Walker, Mary Kennan Herbert, has been wonderful. She helped me through a new and somewhat intimidating experience.

My parents deserve a special thank-you. Their moral support over the past year has been beyond words, and the times they baby-sat will never be forgotten. They have also lived with my writing for many years. It began with poetry at the age of nine, and finally I have made it this far. I think they were the only ones who ever really believed I could do it.

The wonderful people at the Craig Moffat County Library in Craig, Colorado, have been fantastic. Much of the credit for this book should go to them. For all the interlibrary loans, special requests, articles they clipped, and the encouragement and smiles, I thank them from the bottom of my heart. They are a one-in-a-million group, and our little community here in Colorado is lucky to have them.

Even though he has not helped specifically with this book, I must say thank-you to a very special man: Ed Weiss. Ed taught me how to think, to question, to dig a little deeper. He has always had words of encouragement for me, and he believes in me as few people ever could. Without his guidance a few years ago, this book would never have been written.

The biggest thank-yous go to my husband and my son. My six-year-old son, Patrick, has been wonderful at trying to help out. I appreciate that he understands how important it is when Mommy has to write. Bill has been my researcher, my editor, my proofreader, my housekeeper, my cook, my moral support, and my friend through this. He has been understanding and supportive and helps keep me dreaming. He never lets me forget that Vienna is waiting . . .

Foreword

The environmental movement comprises a rich and diverse array of ideas, actions, and philosophies. Uniting the members of this bold social movement is a deep concern for the future of the planet and the millions of species that share their home with us.

Despite this common bond, interest within the movement varies widely. Some organizations focus their energies on protecting wilderness. Others concern themselves with the plight of endangered species. Still others promote clean, renewable energy resources or ways to use resources such as water and energy with greater efficiency, and so on.

At times the diversity of the environmental community seems overwhelming, even to those of us who have been part of the environmental movement for years. While mind-boggling, this diversity is one of the movement's greater strengths. When taken together, the seemingly disparate actions of the environmental movement form a larger strategy—an often unarticulated strategy that advances humanity toward a more sustainable relationship with nature. A sustainable society is one that meets its needs without impairing the ability of future generations to meet theirs. It is a society whose economy exists in harmony with the economy of nature. Such a task requires a broad and diverse approach.

Although the environmental movement spans the constellation of challenges we face as a world community, no one can participate in every facet. We must do our part and trust that others will do theirs.

Doing our part requires individual responsibility and action. *The Nature Directory* explains some of the major environmental problems facing the planet and offers some suggestions for reprioritizing our lives. These simple efforts require surprisingly very little time. But don't be fooled by the simplicity of small actions. When added to the actions of many others, they can make a profound difference.

Individuals can also help by supporting environmental and conservation groups whose interests align with theirs. By giving both time and money, you become an evolutionary force in the transition to a sustainable future.

The Nature Directory can help locate national organizations whose interests overlap with yours. The main body of this book lists many prominent environmental groups working in the United States and abroad to stem the destruction and seek a better balance with nature. It outlines past achievements, ongoing projects, and future plans and describes opportunities for volunteer work. As a resource to those wishing to plug in to the environmental movement, *The Nature Directory* is unequaled. Browse through the entries and then become an active member of the planet Earth's greatest ally, the environmental movement. But don't forget to support state and local organizations as well. Many of their programs are chronically underfunded and understaffed. Individuals can have a great deal of influence at the local level, and a donation of time or money to a state or local organization goes a long way. Many national groups have state offices or chapters in which you can become involved.

United by our common bond of love for the Earth, we can build a sustainable future in a world often blinded with self-interest and greed. We cannot wait for government of business to do it. It is up to us and the time is now.

Daniel D. Chiras
President, Colorado Environmental
Coalition and author of *Beyond the Fray:
Reshaping America's Environmental Response*

Introduction

Albert Schweitzer once said, "Man has lost the capacity to foresee and to forestall. He will end by destroying the earth." Many people see the last decade of the twentieth century as the last chance to prove Dr. Schweitzer wrong. Indeed, the 1990s have already been called the environmental decade by the media. In the United States, change is most evident in the programs being undertaken at the local level. Community recycling is popular in neighborhoods across the country. In areas such as Los Angeles, residents are required to separate trash and to set aside recyclable items. The nation's largest recycler, Waste Management, Inc., recycled nearly 600,000 tons of trash nationwide during 1989.

The summer of 1988 brought terms such as *global warming* and *the greenhouse effect* to households across the United States as temperatures soared and even the mighty Mississippi became a giant mud hole.

In 1987 Burger King was forced to change its meat acquisition policies when a boycott on the fast-food franchise caused sales to plummet.

In July 1988, at the height of the tourist season, the beaches from New Jersey to Long Island closed as waste and medical debris washed ashore.

A barge loaded with 3,000 tons of garbage wandered the seas for months in 1989 as state after state and country after country refused to accept Long Island's trash.

In the spring of 1983 the town of Times Beach, Missouri, ceased to exist. The Environmental Protection Agency (EPA) spent $36.7 million to buy out the dioxin-contaminated town of 2,500 residents.

The list of incidents continues, each one making the public a little more aware of possible disasters lurking just out of sight. The 1980s saw a surge of support for environmental organizations as more horror stories began to surface and the Reagan administration failed to take any significant action to support the environment. In fact, as the EPA was steeped in the controversy surrounding its administrator Anne Burford, and rumors had Interior Secretary James Watt ready to sell off the Grand Canyon to developers, memberships in environmental organizations soared.

The groups most popular and most widely recognized during the 1980s have come to be known collectively as the Group of Ten: Defenders of Wildlife, Environmental Defense Fund, Environmental Policy Institute, Izaak Walton League, National Audubon Society, National Parks and Conservation Association, National Wildlife Federation, Natural Resources Defense Council, Sierra Club, and Wilderness Society.

In addition to the larger organizations, many smaller groups saw a rapid increase in membership during the 1980s, and several new groups developed. Today, some of the most active environmental groups are those with little name recognition. While some have existed for decades, others are the offspring of the Group of Ten: Greenpeace, Earth First! Sea Shepherds, Rainforest Action Network, Earth Island Institute, Citizens' Clearinghouse for Hazardous Wastes.

The Nature Directory gives an overview of environmental organizations. From the large, highly organized to the small grassroots organizations, the directory will provide you with a basic understanding of each organization.

In Part I the environmental problems addressed by the environmental groups are discussed, as well as some of the proposed solutions. Part II is a sampling of 120 environmental groups. In this section, each organization is presented individually with a summary of the group's history, goals, achievements, plans, membership information, and volunteer possibilities within the group. Part III is a guide to personal involvement in the environmental issues. A selected resource list follows Part III including a special guide to children's books on the environment.

The Nature Directory is a guidebook that will take you through the 1990s as Americans discover that environmental concerns continue to escalate.

THE
NATURE
DIRECTORY

ENVIRONMENTAL PROBLEMS

Environmental problems have become the focus of much media attention in recent years. To list all of the environmental problems would take pages; to explain them all and detail their causes, significance, and the ramifications of each would take volumes. Environmental organizations have found it easier to categorize the major problems into broad headings. Because the earth is a single, interdependent ecosystem, all areas of the environment benefit from any successes made in the major areas. The ten most commonly cited environmental problems are: air pollution; acid rain; greenhouse-effect warming and depletion of the ozone layer; chemicals; toxic wastes; garbage (solid waste); destruction of forests; destruction of wilderness areas and wetlands; wildlife extinction; and energy and natural resource depletion.

AIR POLLUTION

Air pollution is the most widely publicized environmental problem. As early as World War I, a brown haze was spotted over Los Angeles. By World War II, the smog was bad enough to sting eyes and make people cough. In 1952, the smog in London was so severe it caused 4,000 deaths. During the drought of 1988, the smog crisis spread across the United States. Not only were the traditionally smog-plagued cities hit with severe ozone pollution levels, but midwestern cities and areas of rural Maine and upstate New York were also seriously affected.

The environmental organizations are working to reduce the amount of pollutants emitted into the air. It is estimated that more than 100 toxic chemicals are legally emitted. While new cars have tougher emission standards, the number of cars on the roads has increased dramatically. The estimated number of miles driven by Americans each year increased by more than 20 percent during the 1980s, effectively negating any progress that could have resulted from the tougher emission standards.

Most environmental organizations believe that part of the solution lies in a strengthened Clean Air Act and even tougher emission standards for all automobiles and factories in the United States.

ACID RAIN

In the decade since scientists first warned Americans that rain and snow are poisoning freshwater streams and ponds through the acid-forming pollutants in the air, studies have shown that the problem may be even worse than suspected.

In their pleas to the public, environmental groups cite scientific studies that find high levels of pollutants in areas of massive forest die-offs. In some areas, forest die-off increased by as much as 30 percent over the last few years of the past decade. States in New England, the worst acid-rain area in the United States, report that most of the water systems are affected. In New York, a recent study reported that 25 percent of the state's lakes and ponds in the Adirondack Mountains are too acidic to support fish. Similar bodies of water were located throughout New England. State officials estimate that within twenty years much of the drinking water in Massachusetts will have lost its ability to fight acidification. Much of the problem is caused by the burning of coal to generate electricity. Especially in the East and northeast, coal is high in sulfur content and produces massive amounts of sulfur dioxide when burned.

In response to acid rain, environmental groups propose tougher standards for sulfur dioxide emissions. One recent proposal would require coal-fired power plants to clean up by installing scrubbers and burning a more expensive, better grade of coal.

GREENHOUSE EFFECT/DEPLETION OF THE OZONE

During the summer of 1988, the world began to listen to warnings about the greenhouse effect as temperatures reached record highs throughout the world. The greenhouse effect is the slow warming of the earth's surface caused when the sun's warm rays become trapped on the earth's surface by large amounts of certain gases, such as carbon dioxide, chlorine, nitrous oxide, and methane, in the atmosphere. These gases act in the same way as panes of glass in a greenhouse. This increase in the average temperature can cause changes in the weather patterns, such as severe drought and raised sea levels. By the end of June 1988, the U.S. Soil Conservation Service estimated that 750,000 acres of farmland in Montana, Wyoming, and the Dakotas had lost its topsoil, blown away in the high winds. Fires destroyed thousands of acres in the West, including large parcels of Yellowstone National Park. Barges sat stranded on the Mississippi as the mighty river became a gigantic mud flat.

Equally alarming to environmentalists is the rapid depletion of the ozone layer. This layer of the earth's atmosphere prevents excessive amounts of ultraviolet radiation from reaching the earth's surface. As the ozone layer decreases, more ultraviolet rays reach earth, causing increased incidence of skin cancer and cataracts and a weakening of the body's immune system.

Environmental organizations target several culprits of the greenhouse effect and ozone depletion: deforestation and burning of trees; chlorofluorocarbons (CFCs) in aerosols, plastics, air conditioning, etc.; energy use and production; industry practices; and agriculture.

One of the biggest efforts on the part of environmentalists is to decrease deforestation. Trees absorb carbon dioxide and produce oxygen. Fires produce carbon dioxide. When people cut down trees and burn off large areas for development, not only is the original function of the trees affected, but extra carbon dioxide is also produced by the burning, intensifying the problem.

The CFCs used in aerosol cans, plastics, and coolants are another problem that many groups are actively attacking. In 1978 the use of CFCs in spray cans was banned in the United States. Some fast-food franchises have been targeted for their use of CFC-containing foam packages. In the cities of Berkeley, California, and Portland, Oregon, it is actually illegal for restaurants to use the foam containers. Many groups encourage a boycott of industries still utilizing the CFC-containing plastics.

Factory emissions responsible for the problems of air pollution and acid rain have also been found to contain large amounts of carbon dioxide. Environmental organizations have been lobbying Congress for new laws to curtail current factory emissions.

Energy conservation is a major concern to many environmentalists. The average U.S. car, according to Environmental Action, creates fifty-seven tons of carbon dioxide in its lifetime. Environmentalists encourage bicycling and walking or using public transportation systems instead of private automobiles. The groups have also strongly lobbied to increase the Corporate Average Fuel Economy (CAFE) standard for U.S. automobiles. The 1990 standard, after numerous rollbacks throughout the Reagan years, is 27.5 mpg. A goal of many environmental groups is a CAFE standard of 45 mpg by the year 2000.

CHEMICALS

In her 1962 book *Silent Spring*, Rachel Carson shocked the world with her alarming revelation about the effect of pesticides and other chemicals on the environment. Since then, the gravity of the problem has been the focus of much debate and a key concern of environmentalists.

In 1988 reports of Alar on apples were the focus of the public's attention. Chemicals on food became a concern for a majority of Americans. The sale of organic products doubled during the 1980s.

Pesticides are increasingly linked to cancer and other ailments. Farmers who use pesticides have been found to be at high risk. The National Cancer Institute reported that farmers in Kansas who used 2,4-D, a popular weed killer found in over-the-counter products, had a risk seven times higher than average of contracting non-Hodgkin's lymphoma, a rare form of cancer.

Every year in the United States over 300 million pounds of pesticides are applied to lawns, gardens, parks, and golf courses. To reduce the use of these chemicals, environmental organizations are promoting alternatives such as biological pest controls.

Across the country, groups at the local level have been formed to function as a type of community watchdog committee over pesticide producers and large-scale users. The environmental organizations are working to let the public know that a controversy exists, to educate people about the possible effects of chemicals, and to offer safer alternatives.

TOXIC WASTE

The 1980s brought headline reports of entire cities disappearing after toxic wastes were discovered dumped and abandoned. The city of Times Beach, Missouri, was abandoned after toxic waste burial sites were discovered. The name Love Canal became synonymous with horror and fear.

In 1976 Congress passed the Resource Conservation and Recovery Act. The RCRA directed the Environmental Protection Agency to establish landfill regulations and a system for tracking hazardous wastes. In 1980 the EPA finally issued the regulations after threats of court action over the delays. The RCRA was strengthened by a 1984 amendment, and The Comprehensive Environmental Response, Compensation and Liability Act of 1980, or the Superfund Program, administered by the EPA, was established to help citizens clean up sites already contaminated.

The emphasis of many environmental groups is on eliminating the problem at the source rather than dealing with it after the fact. A demand for toxic waste reduction is so far being met with resistance by industry. As late as 1986 nearly 50 percent of the companies producing toxic wastes had not implemented waste-reduction procedures. Environmentalists continue to lobby for tougher standards and tighter controls.

GARBAGE

Every year Americans throw away 160 million tons of garbage, an 80 percent increase since 1960 and the largest amount of any country in the world. Although families across the nation now recycle 11 percent of all their trash, they still throw out a little over 3.5 pounds of trash per person per day, according to the EPA. More terrifying is the fact that the EPA expects that figure to increase to an estimated 2,300 pounds of garbage per person annually over the next decade. At the same time, landfills across the country are filling up. Only one-third of the nation's landfills from 20 years ago are still open, and another one-third of those are expected to reach capacity before 1995.

Environmentalists warned of the problem nearly two decades ago. Today they are still encouraging recycling and have backed bills making recycling mandatory when volunteer efforts failed.

Across the country, local and state officials are calling for changes. In the country's most ambitious ordinance, Minneapolis-St. Paul, Minnesota, passed a law allowing only recyclable packaging on store shelves. Florida put a 10¢ per ton tax on nonrecycled newsprint. High Bridge, New Jersey, instituted a pay-by-the-bag trash disposal system. Residents pay $140 a year, which enables them to dump one thirty-gallon bag of trash each week; additional bags cost residents $1.25 each. In Los Angeles County, recycling is now mandatory. In six states it is illegal to dump yard wastes into landfills.

As the problem becomes more widely recognized, environmentalists are encouraging actions such as: composting household scraps and lawn debris; separating glass, plastic, aluminum cans, and newspaper; buying products with as little packaging as possible and large size packages of products; the use of cloth diapers instead of the estimated 28 billion disposable diapers used yearly across the United States; and avoiding the use of plastic plates, cups, paper towels, and other disposable products.

DESTRUCTION OF FORESTS

The trees have always held a kind of mystery for humankind. Under a tree is the ideal place to sit and contemplate the wonders of the universe. The fruit from some trees can satisfy the heartiest appetite. A tree can provide cool shade in summer or block the winds of a winter storm. Yet trees do so much more for our world than many people realize. Trees use the carbon dioxide that contributes to the greenhouse effect and give back oxygen in return. Trees hold the topsoil in place to prevent desertification. The Douglas fir forests of the Cascade Range in the Pacific Northwest contain 264,000 gallons of water per acre, which protects the animals from harsh winters. Yet every year 2.8 billion trees are cut down worldwide, and the United States ranks first in the number of trees logged.

Clear-cutting trees, many argue, irreparably destroys the ecological system and leads eventually to desertification. Ethiopia is a stark example of what many environmentalists see in store for the United States. Though it was once covered by grass and trees, overgrazing, deforestation, and drought conditions turned Ethiopia into a desert of starving people. The United Nations estimates that 80,000 square miles of land across the globe become desert each year.

A major concern of environmental groups is the tropical rain forests. A 1982 report by the U.S. National Academy of Sciences estimated that a four-square-mile section of rain forest may contain 750 species of trees, 125 kinds of mammals, 400 types of birds, 100 kinds of reptiles and 60 different types of amphibians. In 1988 alone an estimated 12,350 square miles of Brazilian rain forest were destroyed, mostly by fires that were set to clear the land for crops and development. In fact an estimated 2 to 5 percent of the earth's surface is set on fire each year to clear land for agriculture.

One of the immediate problems caused by deforestation is the effect on the earth's temperatures. Every year, 5.2 billion tons of carbon are emitted into the atmosphere from the burning of fossil fuels; another 1.8 billion tons come from burning tropical forests. Not only are there more air pollutants, but the crucial role the trees play in the ecosystem is greatly altered.

The environmental organizations are fighting hard to save the forests. Massive reforestation projects have been introduced. The groups are encouraging farsighted plans that aim at managing forests better.

In a novel approach to preserving rain forests, several groups have begun land-for-debt swaps in which huge sections of forest are turned over to the environmental group for administration and protection in return for a payoff of part of the country's debt.

WILDERNESS AREAS

As populations soared and expanded, the indigenous animals in many areas across the country became extinct when their homelands disappeared. In recent years, environmental organizations have pushed the government to designate large areas as wilderness areas. Not only are the animals in such areas protected but the entire ecosystem is allowed to remain as close to the natural state as possible. This means no mining, no oil and gas exploration, no motorized vehicles. In many preserves the number of people and the areas to which they have access are carefully controlled.

The environmental groups lobby Congress for designate greater areas as wildlands. In some instances, the organizations themselves buy up large tracts of land containing unique ecosystems and designate the area as a wilderness preserve.

WILDLIFE EXTINCTION

As the wilderness and wetlands disappeared, so too have the wild inhabitants of these areas. One of the most popular campaigns, stretching back to the 1960s, was the campaign to save the whales. This action brought the 1972 U.S. Marine Mammal Protection Act and the 1973 U.S. Endangered Species Act, which protected whales in U.S. waters and made the importation of whale products illegal. Other countries such as Japan, Iceland, and Norway, however, continue to hunt and kill thousands of whales each year.

During the 1988 drought many struggling species finally gave in to environmental pressures. Especially hard hit were the inhabitants of wetlands. Every year 300,000 to 500,000 acres of wetlands are drained for development. The combination of this dwindling of their natural habitats and the extreme drought conditions caused fish populations to drop dramatically; duck migrations hit record lows.

According to a 1988 report by Defenders of Wildlife, 500 species are endangered and another 4,000 are threatened in the United States alone. It has been predicted that by the year 2000, entire species of plants and animals will become extinct across the world at a rate of one per minute.

Environmental organizations have staged massive campaigns to protect wildlife and, where necessary, to reintroduce species into wilderness areas. Many new refuges and habitats are being established and indigenous animals reintroduced into the areas. One popular program involves wolves, which are being reintroduced into native areas such as Yellowstone National Park, coastal areas of North Carolina, and a new location in Colorado.

Many organizations continue to promote the humane treatment of wildlife and to encourage people to boycott furs and fur manufacturers. Boycotts against tuna companies have been successful in reducing the unnecessary killing of dolphins that swim with the tuna. The organizations hope to effect some real changes in the treatment of and respect for wild animals and the wilderness areas in which they live by increasing public awareness of the situation.

ENERGY AND NATURAL RESOURCE DEPLETION

The issue of energy conservation becomes a focus for Americans during periods of crisis when world oil prices skyrocket. In times of lower prices, energy consumption is rarely mentioned, and the availability of energy supplies is taken for granted. Environmental organizations are attempting to show Americans that there are other reasons to stop and consider the amount of energy they utilize daily.

Not only does an excessive demand for energy deplete the earth's natural resources, but energy use is seen as a major contributor to a variety of other environmental problems—acid rain, pollution, global warming.

The world's high demand for energy, currently derived primarily from fossil fuels, is causing the depletion of these fossil fuels at a rate 100,000 times faster than the fuels are being formed.

The cost to the environment of such excessive uses of energy is high, according to many environmentalists. The largest percentage of carbon dioxide in the atmosphere is caused by the burning of fossil fuels in automobiles, power plants, and factories. Even though the data is not yet conclusive, it is believed that half of all global warming is caused by carbon dioxide.

To reduce the threat to the environment and preserve natural resources, environmental organizations have offered a range of alternatives. Greater research into solar and wind power is often called for. Organizations encourage energy efficiency at home, from using lower wattage bulbs and fluorescent bulbs to lowering thermostats and buying more efficient appliances. Finding alternatives to automobiles and using public transportation are encouraged. Many of the organizations have called for more fuel efficient cars. Current technologies, according to some experts, would allow for fuel efficiency levels of approximately 60 miles per gallon. The Natural Resources Defense Council estimates that even a 45 mpg standard would reduce carbon dioxide emissions in the United States by 15 percent. The organizations have so far met with strong resistance from the auto industry and oil producers.

The organizations all pledge to continue to work toward educating the public and toward enacting higher energy-efficiency standards for automobiles and industry emissions.

HOW THE ORGANIZATIONS BRING ABOUT CHANGE

Environmental organizations range from passive to active in their response to various problems. Some utilize a variety of methods, while others have found one approach that works best for their goals.

Among the more traditional methods are boycotting, letter writing, and civil disobedience. If mass public support is available for a cause, boycotts prove successful. Boycotts have been utilized in cases involving the meat acquisition policies of Burger King, the methods of tuna fishing that also kill large numbers of dolphins, the whaling practices of countries such as Japan, Iceland, and Norway. Letter writing is used by most organizations as a supplementary action. Many times if there is a bill before Congress that relates to a particular organization's goals, members will be encouraged to write to their senators, representatives, and even the president. Civil disobedience has become more popular as the attention of the media has increased. Visual tactics to demonstrate a point have included such actions as members' sitting in front of logging equipment, chaining themselves to equipment, wearing furs with a bloodlike substance dripping from them, sitting in trees, and putting banners on nuclear power plants. The list continues but the main idea remains constant: a visual action is taken, but nothing is done to harm other people or property.

As environmental organizations have grown and their budgets become larger, the groups have begun to use the courts and the legislatures to accomplish their goals. All of the largest organizations have lobbyists in Washington who work full-time to push the agenda of their respective organizations through Congress. Many groups also have lobbyists at the state level who work to create local policies. Litigation is also an option for many organizations as the courts have become a battleground for environmental issues. The Sierra Club Legal Defense Fund, a nonprofit organization employing nearly thirty attorneys in six offices across the country, has hundreds of environmental organizations as clients and originates numerous lawsuits and administrative actions on their behalf each year.

Various preservation and management programs also account for much of the action taken by environmental organizations. The debt-for-nature swaps with indebted Third World countries have become popular. Direct purchasing of land, and subsequently preserving and managing it, is an option for the larger groups. Educating the general public on environmental problems and solutions is another would-be remedy offered by some groups, usually in combination with other more active programs. Joint programs with government agencies and corporate representatives are also popular with some groups, although many of the smaller grass-roots organizations frown on this type of bureaucracy.

The most controversial environmental tactic is ecoterrorism.

Ecoterrorism ranges from vandalism and sabotage to theft or beyond. Done in the name of the environment and under the assumption that human beings are only one more link in the chain of life—no more nor less important than any other—ecoterrorism has included breaking into buildings and vandalizing the interiors, cutting fences and electrical wires, spiking trees to prevent logging, destroying the engines of bulldozers by adding sugar to gas tanks, slashing tires, setting off homemade bombs and Molotov cocktails, cutting fishing nets, stealing laboratory animals, and even sinking whaling ships and destroying factories.

Whatever tactics you believe are most effective and most compatible with your own goals, you should carefully check the organizations you are interested in to see not only what causes they fight for, but how they fight.

ENVIRONMENTAL ORGANIZATIONS

Included in this section are 120 environmental organizations. They are listed in alphabetical order, and the same information is provided about each for easy reference.

If the organization is large and has several or many smaller chapters, the address and phone number given is that of the national or main office.

Most of the information given is extracted from material sent out by the individual organizations, although some general information may come from other published sources and news stories.

The profile provided is only a brief summary of what is, in some instances, volumes of information. The summary will, however, give you the necessary information to choose which organizations you would like to study further and to eliminate those groups with which you share few or no common goals. Each section concludes with an overview of membership benefits and describes ways in which to become involved with the organization.

☐ AFRICAN WILDLIFE FOUNDATION
1717 Massachusetts Avenue, NW
Washington, DC 20036
(202) 265-8393
Contact: Paul T. Schindler, President

History/Goals
The African Wildlife Foundation was founded in 1961 to protect African wildlife. Since its founding, AWF has had an office in Nairobi, Kenya, to promote the idea that the Africans themselves are best equipped to protect African wildlife. There are currently 100,000 AWF members worldwide.

Past Achievements

African Wildlife Foundation established two colleges of wildlife management in Tanzania and Cameroon to provide environmental training in Africa.

AWF has provided a radio communication network in Africa, as well as several airplanes and vehicles for antipoaching patrols in the Tsavo Sanctuary working in conjunction with Dr. Richard Leakey.

The African Wildlife Foundation and the Kenya Wildlife Service and Department of Adult Education published *Let's Conserve Our Wildlife*. This book, written in Swahili, includes teachers' guides and is being used in adult literacy classes sponsored by various African governments.

Ongoing Projects

A pilot project entitled "Protected Areas: Neighbors as Partners" in Tanzania at the edge of the Serengeti National Park is attempting to illustrate the benefits the local people receive when nearby areas are protected. The program points out the balance between land conservation and the needs of people and livestock in the surrounding areas.

A major three-year project was launched in Tanzania by AWF in 1990 in conjunction with the World Wildlife Fund. The Planning and Assessment for Wildlife Management project, funded by the U.S. Agency for International Development, is designed to provide technical assistance to the Ministry of Lands, Natural Resources, and Tourism and is aimed at upgrading the Tanzanian Wildlife Division.

AWF's Elephant Awareness Campaign has been one of its most successful to date. The popular slogan "Only Elephants Should Wear Ivory" has helped gain widespread media exposure for AWF, has attracted many additional members, and has made the public aware of the plight of the elephants.

AWF also supports education centers, over 1,000 wildlife clubs, and a number of youth hostels located in national parks.

Future Plans

Conservation education was the original focus of the African Wildlife Foundation and continues to be its primary focus today. AWF is setting up a new course at the College of African Wildlife Management in Tanzania. This course will allow students to learn community conservation activities and will help park authorities in learning to work with those residents living adjacent to protected areas.

AWF continues to assist in the management of several wildlife parks and reserves and helps government agencies in Africa develop land-use plans and improve national park systems.

Membership Information and Volunteer Possibilities

Annual membership in AWF is $25. Members receive the quarterly magazine, *Wildlife News*, to keep up-to-date on activities within the foundation. AWF also offers African safaris to its members.

Although there are no direct volunteer positions within the organization, AWF does send out a "How You Can Help" newsletter to members, giving them hints on how they can help keep the demand for ivory low.

☐ AIR AND WASTE MANAGEMENT ASSOCIATION

P.O. Box 2861
Pittsburgh, PA 15230
(412) 232-3444
Contact: Jon Fedorka

History/Goals

The Air and Waste Management Association was organized in 1907 as the International Association for the Prevention of Smoke. In 1988 the organization changed its name to better reflect its focus and goals in the 1990s. The association is a nonprofit, scientific, educational, and technical organization that promotes a clean environment. Today there are over 11,000 members in fifty countries around the world. The association provides a forum through meetings and publications to examine all aspects of an environmental issue: technical, economic, social, and political.

The association conducts seminars, workshops, conferences, and continuing education courses. It produces *The Journal of the Air & Waste Management Association,* as well as a variety of periodicals, books, management guides, and training manuals.

Past Achievements

The A&WMA has a scholarship endowment fund which, between 1986 and 1989, awarded fourteen scholarships totaling $36,000 to graduate students pursuing careers in fields related to pollution control and waste management.

Ongoing Projects

The association offers specialty conferences, including an annual conference in which members and other environmental professionals meet to exchange data, research findings, and information. Usually ten to twelve other conferences are held each year. One conference offered in 1990 was "How Clean Is Clean? Cleanup Criteria for Contaminated Soil and Groundwater"; it included representatives from government, industry, academia, and consulting groups.

The association also offers government affairs seminars in Washington, D.C., and Ottawa, Ontario, Canada. Annually, five to ten short workshops are sponsored providing details and information on a particular topic.

Future Plans

The association sees training seminars as one of the major areas of growth. In 1990 a task force was formed to help formulate training programs for the future.

The association also plans to develop public outreach programs for schoolchildren and the general public.

Membership Information and Volunteer Possibilities

The Air and Waste Management Association is an all-volunteer organization. The association has twenty-one sections across the country, allowing members to meet at the regional level to discuss regional and even local environmental issues. While the A&WMA is primarily a professional organization for those active in the field of waste management, it has sponsored essay contests, science fairs, picnics, and community activities, and makes speakers available to address high school and college students.

A&WMA's membership year runs from May 1 through April 30; dues are $75. Membership includes a subscription to both the association journal and the bimonthly newsletter, and a copy of the membership directory.

☐ THE ALLIANCE TO SAVE ENERGY

1725 K Street, NW, Suite 914
Washington, DC 20006-1401
(202) 857-0666
Contact: James L. Wolf, Executive Director

History/Goals

The Alliance to Save Energy is a coalition of business, government, environmental, and consumer leaders. The alliance's major goal is the increased efficiency of energy use. The alliance conducts research, organizes pilot projects, conducts educational programs, and formulates policy initiatives.

The chairman of the board of directors is Senator Timothy Wirth (D-Colo.). The board also includes representatives from labor unions, utility companies, defense contractors, other environmental organizations, and the Harvard Business School.

Past Achievements

In Arkansas, Colorado, and Maine, the alliance brought together utility companies and state agencies to set up joint programs on economic development and low-income assistance projects.

The alliance has launched a major consumer education campaign aimed at presenting energy-efficient alternatives to consumers. Advertisements on energy efficiency have appeared in general interest magazines, and guides to efficient lighting have been distributed nationwide.

Ongoing Projects

The alliance promotes energy efficiency as a way to reduce housing costs and make affordable housing available to low-income renters and first-time home buyers. To reduce these costs, the alliance is pushing five policies: creation of a uniform mortgage policy to encourage the purchase of energy-efficient homes; upgrading the energy standards for federally assisted housing; institution of a home energy rating system nationwide; developing incentives in housing assistance programs for energy efficiency; and the reduction, through conservation, of energy costs in public housing.

The alliance continuously conducts workshops, forums, and training sessions. Experts from the alliance testify before Congress and for the courts. Policy studies, technical manuals, and computer software are developed for industry leaders, and booklets and pamphlets are distributed to consumers and educators.

Future Plans

The alliance believes that energy efficiency can help achieve vital national goals such as environmental protection, affordable housing, national security, economic development, and international competitiveness. To further these objectives, the alliance formulates policy and works closely with industry and government agencies to implement these policies. For example, in conjunction with the International Institute for Energy Conservation, the alliance is developing a business roundtable to identify ways for businesses and government to export more energy efficient products.

Membership Information and Volunteer Possibilities

Support for the alliance comes from corporations, foundations, governments, utilities, businesses, unions, and individual consumers. Annual membership is $25.

The alliance is an excellent source of reference material on energy conservation. The alliance publishes materials covering a wide range of topics—economics, consumer conservation, utility conservation, industrial conservation, and topic papers on individual issues.

☐ AMERICAN BIRDING ASSOCIATION
P.O. Box 6599
Colorado Springs, CO 80934-6599
(800) 634-7736
Contacts: Cindy Lippincott, Manager
Bob Berman, Comanager

History/Goals

The American Birding Association was founded over twenty years ago and is dedicated to helping Americans increase their enjoyment of birds. To accomplish this goal, the association helps members strengthen identification skills, enriches bird-finding ability, and helps keep members informed about resources, publications, and new equipment.

Past Achievements
The American Birding Association has developed an extensive catalog of publications and equipment available to members and nonmembers. Members receive discounts on certain catalog items.

Ongoing Projects
ABA holds a biennial convention open to all members. This week-long meeting consists of workshops, speakers, and field trips with expert guides. Meetings are held in different cities throughout the United States.

ABA sponsors birding weekends and tours on an ongoing basis throughout the year. Trips are to both foreign and domestic locations and are conducted by experienced tour guides.

Future Plans
ABA plans to continue offering its members a broad range of publications and birding items, as well as the ABA weekends and ABA trips.

Membership Information and Volunteer Possibilities
Annual membership in the American Birding Association is $24. There is a family rate available of $30 annually and a lifetime membership of $500. Members receive a copy of ABA's bimonthly magazine, *Birding*, along with a monthly newsletter entitled *Winging It*, featuring news for members, bird-finding information, and classified advertisements. Members also receive a copy of the membership directory, which helps them stay in touch across the country.

Although there are no formal volunteer opportunities within the organization, members are eligible to attend the biennial convention and can join ABA trips and weekends.

☐ AMERICAN CAVE CONSERVATION ASSOCIATION

Main & Cave Street
P.O. Box 409
Horse Cave, KY 42749
(502) 786-1466
Contacts: David Goster, Executive Director
Judy Petersen, Education Director

History/Goals
The American Cave Conservation Association was founded in 1977 to protect and preserve caves, karstlands, and groundwater. The association currently has 500 members and is most active in its hometown of Horse Cave, Kentucky.

Past Achievements
ACCA works closely with the public to develop information and an awareness of caves, sinkholes, and underground streams (known as karstland). The association brought a Keep America Beautiful program

to Hart County, Kentucky, and began an Adopt-a-Highway program in the same county.

ACCA has worked with the Tennessee Nature Conservancy on projects at New Mammoth and Pearson's caves.

Ongoing Projects

Annually, ACCA holds a Cave Management Training Seminar in cooperation with the USDA Forest Service.

ACCA is currently in the process of constructing the American Cave and Karst Center, the country's first museum devoted specifically to caves and karstland.

The association sponsors a River Cleanup of the Green River in Hart County, Kentucky, where the ACCA offices are located. The group's education director gives in-service presentations to teachers in Hart County concerning recycling and solid waste disposal, and offers a slide show on the subject for groups and schools across the country.

Future Plans

ACCA is working to develop a national clearinghouse of information on caves and karstland. In 1989 ACCA processed 200 requests for information and expanded its library 25 percent.

Membership Information and Volunteer Possibilities

ACCA focuses on providing complete and accurate information to the public. Educational programs are geared toward schoolchildren as well as professional land managers. An educational director works with schools and the community to develop curriculum materials.

Regular membership in the association is $25; student members pay $12, and life members $350. Each member receives *American Caves*, the ACCA magazine, discounts on ACCA publications, and invitations to special events, projects, and meetings.

☐ AMERICAN CETACEAN SOCIETY

P.O. Box 2639
San Pedro, CA 90731
(213) 548-6279
Contact: Patricia Warhol, Executive Director

History/Goals

The American Cetacean Society was founded in 1967 as a whale protection group. ACS has nine chapters in the United States in addition to the national headquarters in San Pedro, California. The organization of whale enthusiasts, marine scientists, and educators works in the areas of education, research, and conservation to protect whales and dolphins. There are currently 2,700 members.

Past Achievements

American Cetacean Society has developed resource materials useful to teachers, such as the "Gray Whale Teaching Kit" and the "Whale Fact

Pack". A cetacean research library was established at the national head-quarters and is open to the public.

Ongoing Projects

ACS has an active education program. The organization distributes free information on request, trains boat skippers and whale watch docents, and continues to develop educational tools for the classroom.

ACS supports marine mammal research and funds various researchers. A biennial conference allows researchers, conservationists, and the public to exchange information and ideas on issues concerning whales.

An ACS representative lives in Washington, D.C., and continuously monitors legislation and attends meetings of the International Whaling Commission. The representative also serves as a liaison between ACS and other wildlife organizations on issues pertaining to whales and the ocean.

Future Plans

American Cetacean Society continues to educate the public on issues concerning the whales of the world and the oceans in which they live. The organization will continue to organize meetings, send representatives to various conferences, and work in the legislative process to bring about changes in activities that currently threaten whales and their habitat.

Membership Information and Volunteer Possibilities

Annual membership in ACS is $25 and includes a subscription to *Whalewatcher*, the ACS quarterly journal, and a subscription to *Whale-News*, the ACS newsletter. Members also receive discounts on whale watching trips and can be affiliated with one of nine local chapters, located in Galveston, Texas; Los Angeles, California; Monterey, California; Orange County, California; San Diego, California; Santa Barbara, California; Santa Monica, California; Seattle, Washington; and New York/New Jersey. The local chapters have chapter newsletters and sponsor activities for the members. Members are encouraged to write letters to Congress. Various programs in the chapters include activities such as "Adopt-a-Dolphin" programs and beach cleanups. Members may attend seminars and help in ACS-sponsored programs or programs in affiliated organizations.

☐ AMERICAN FARMLAND TRUST

1920 N Street, NW, Suite 400
Washington, DC 20036
(202) 659-5170
Contact: Ralph Grossi, President

History/Goals

The American Farmland Trust was founded in 1980 to help develop policies aimed at protecting land held by private farmers. AFT has

20,000 members and works closely with farmers, businesspeople, legislators, and conservationists.

AFT's major goal is to develop the most effective ways to keep land in production.

Past Achievements

Since 1980, AFT has helped protect 26,000 acres of farmland in nineteen states. In 1989, AFT rescued the 507-acre Murray Farm on Michigan's Old Mission Peninsula when this farm of cherry orchards became threatened with a vacation home development.

AFT worked with The Nature Conservancy to protect 300 acres of farm and wetlands in Virginia's Tidewater region in the Chesapeake Bay watershed.

The Illinois Sustainable Agriculture Society (ISAS) was established in cooperation with the State of Illinois. This group of Illinois farmers is devoted to developing and learning about resource-conserving farming methods.

Ongoing Projects

The American Farmland Trust conducts workshops nationwide to help reach farmers and discuss conservation programs and farming methods.

AFT provides expert testimony at congressional and public hearings to present the farmers' perspective on development projects and to try to protect America's farmland.

Future Plans

AFT has recently begun expanding its outreach program. "Seed for the Future" kits, developed in 1989, are expected to reach children nationwide. The program teaches children the benefits of agriculture and helps each child grow a plant.

AFT has begun a multiyear program to assist farmers and local governments in California's Central Valley in protecting agricultural land from encroaching development.

Membership Information and Volunteer Possibilities

Membership in American Farmland Trust is $15 annually and includes a subscription to the quarterly newsletter.

AFT utilizes both grassroots activists as well as lobbyists in Washington, D.C., in its campaigns. Members are encouraged to work at the local level to prevent development of farmland, whether it is their own land or belongs to someone else in the community.

☐ THE AMERICAN HIKING SOCIETY

1015 31st Street, NW, 4th Floor
Washington, DC 20007–4490
(202) 385-3252
Contact: Susan A. Henley, Executive Director

History/Goals

The American Hiking Society was founded in 1977 by hikers concerned that the nation's footpaths were in danger. AHS works with federal agencies to help them best serve the public. The society also works with Congress to influence the federal budget and policies in both the executive and legislative branches of government.

Past Achievements

AHS has worked with Congress to get a portion of the Bureau of Land Management's budget designated for trails. Until 1987, no money was spent on trails. AHS's work has also resulted in an increase in the amount budgeted by the National Park Service for trails.

The American Hiking Society has been successful in acquiring funding from Congress to help in the conversion of abandoned railroad right-of-ways into trails.

Ongoing Projects

AHS participates in the National Trails Coalition. This coalition of national groups (Sierra Club, the Wilderness Society, and the National Audubon Society) helps to raise the public's awareness of threats to trails. The coalition also sponsors a lobbying week during which local activists are brought together in Washington, D.C. to be trained in dealing with the government and informed about national trails issues.

AHS provides information to the public all across the United States. To date, over 40,000 "Hiking Safety" brochures have been distributed. Information requests have doubled at AHS, and the organization now answers over twenty-five requests a day. Twice each year, AHS publishes *Helping Out in the Outdoors,* a directory listing internships and volunteer jobs open to the public throughout the United States.

Future Plans

The American Hiking Society plans to continue its cooperative efforts with federal agencies and Congress. AHS plans to develop programs designed to inform the public, educate trail users in conservation and preservation issues, and to increase volunteer trail building and maintenance.

Membership Information and Volunteer Possibilities

Membership has grown rapidly in recent years. For instance, in fiscal 1989, AHS membership increased 75 percent over the previous year.

Annual membership is $25, with special rates for seniors/students and families. A life membership in AHS is $500. Members receive *American Hiker,* the quarterly magazine; a newsletter published eight times per year; and legislative alerts on issues affecting hikers and trails. Volunteers also receive *Pathways Across America,* a quarterly newsletter published in conjunction with the National Park Service.

AHS members are encouraged to be trail volunteers. AHS's Volunteer Vacations Program sends teams of volunteer trails enthusiasts from across the country to public lands where work is needed on the trails. In 1989 AHS sent out twenty-nine teams made up of nearly 300 volunteers to work sites for two-week stays.

☐ AMERICAN HORSE PROTECTION ASSOCIATION

1000 29th Street, NW, Suite T-100
Washington, DC 20007
(202) 965-0500
Contact: Robin C. Lohnes, Executive Director

History/Goals
The American Horse Protection Association was established in 1966 to promote the welfare of horses and other equine animals, both wild and domestic.

The AHPA has five major goals: to preserve and protect America's wild horses and burros; to prevent the abuse of horses in competition; to assist agencies and individuals in the care of neglected and abused horses; to promote safe transportation of horses; and to educate the public in proper horse care. AHPA accomplishes these goals through litigation, investigation, and public awareness programs.

Past Achievements
AHPA has supported legislation to improve the working conditions of carriage and cart horses and is a member of the D.C. Coalition to Ban Carriage Horses, which seeks to ban carriage horses from the District of Columbia.

In 1989 AHPA filed suit to set aside the regulations allowing the use of 6-ounce action devices in the show ring and the use of pads to build up a horse's front hooves.

During the 1989 Chincoteague pony penning and auction, AHPA distributed foal care packets containing vitamin supplements and instructions on proper foal care. AHPA also monitored horse auctions in Front Royal and Marshall, Virginia, to investigate alleged abuses and violations of anticruelty laws.

Ongoing Projects
The American Horse Protection Association provides assistance and advice as necessary to individuals and groups across the country regarding animal cruelty and abuse.

AHPA continues to operate its 26-acre farm north of Leesburg, Virginia, which houses horses until proper homes can be found for them. Educational programs at the farm feature videos on horse care and introduce the public to America's horses and burros. Tours of the farm are conducted throughout the year for the general public.

An annual Summer Jubilee in Virginia provides the association with the opportunity to distribute information, display a variety of posters and videotapes, answer questions, and attract new members.

Future Plans

The American Horse Protection Association continues to conduct investigations nationally at horse shows, wild horse and burro roundups, auction houses, or wherever they believe there may be abusive treatment of animals.

AHPA continues its work to preserve and protect wild horses and burros on the public lands managed by the U.S. Department of the Interior. AHPA also works with state and federal legislative bodies to ensure the humane treatment of equines.

Membership Information and Volunteer Possibilities

Membership in AHPA is $15 annually. Reduced memberships are available for youths and seniors at $5, and a life membership is available for $500. One-third of all AHPA members are horse owners, trainers, or breeders. Members receive the quarterly newsletter and special alert bulletins. AHPA is also a useful resource for members who have specific questions on the treatment and care of horses.

The AHPA network of volunteers is organized under a state representative program. There are currently sixty-one state representatives in thirty-two states. These members volunteer their time to work at the state level for the humane treatment of horses. For example, in 1989 AHPA volunteers in Colorado cared for 115 horses and placed many of them in adoptive homes. State representatives monitor activities in their local area, distribute AHPA information, and encourage new membership in the organization. Some representatives carry out rescue and placement work, and do fund-raising at the state level.

☐ AMERICAN HUMANE ASSOCIATION

9725 E. Hampden Avenue
Denver, CO 80231
(303) 695-0811
Contact: Office Manager

History/Goals

The American Humane Association was founded in 1877 to prevent neglect, abuse, cruelty, and exploitation in the treatment of animals. The association continues with these same goals today and works to assure that animals' well-being and interests are fully guaranteed.

Past Achievements

The AHA has established the animal protection division. This division is a national federation of over 3,600 local and state animal care agencies and individuals. The division undertakes programs to prevent cruelty, neglect, and abuse of animals.

Ongoing Projects

AHA works to promote quality standards for animal shelters and to reduce euthanasia rates in those shelters. The association maintains education programs for children and adults to show them the responsible way to care for pets. The motion picture industry is continually monitored to ensure that animals are treated properly. The AHA/Delta Society National Hearing Dog Resource Center coordinates and distributes information on the training of unwanted dogs for deaf and hearing-impaired people.

Future Plans

The American Humane Association lobbies for legislation to prevent the abuse of pets, laboratory animals, zoo animals, farm animals, and circus and rodeo animals. Members receive legislative alerts informing them of animal welfare legislation tracked by the association.

Membership Information and Volunteer Possibilities

The AHA educates the public in the humane treatment of animals and has local members of the Animal Protection Division nationwide.

Individuals may join the AHA for a donation of as little as $15. Organizations may join by becoming a supporting agency for $25. Members receive a year's subscription to *The Advocate,* legislative alerts, and a 15 percent discount on publications and posters.

☐ AMERICAN LITTORAL SOCIETY

Sandy Hook
Highlands, NJ 07732
(201) 291-0055
Contact: D. W. Bennett, Executive Director

History/Goals

The American Littoral Society is an organization of professional and amateur naturalists established in 1961 by a group of divers, naturalists, and fishermen. ALS seeks to promote a better understanding of the littoral zone—America's shores and adjacent wetlands, bays, and rivers— and to present a cohesive, unified policy advocating the protection of the littoral zone, including both land and animals.

The society has approximately 9,000 members and serves them through seven regional offices (including two new offices, one in New England and the other serving the West Coast from Washington State) and an ALS affiliate: the Watershed Association of the Delaware River.

Past Achievements

In 1989, ALS established a baykeeper for the New York/New Jersey Harbor to monitor the harbor.

Ongoing Projects

The society runs coastal field trips on an ongoing basis to give members a chance to experience and enjoy the littoral zones the society seeks to protect.

In order to promote protection of the coastal areas, ALS uses a variety of methods, including education of the general public, testimony before Congress and state legislatures, and court actions.

The society works with environmental coalitions to help achieve its goals and is a member of the Coast Alliance, The Barrier Island Coalition, The Society of Wetland Scientists, Monitor, Clean Ocean Action, and various state coalitions.

Future Plans

ALS has been working with the Coast Alliance to develop a plan to force the Environmental Protection Agency to work on developing and enforcing standards for cooling water intake and discharge at hydroelectric power plants.

The society is developing new field trips for its members, such as a driving and hiking trip in Iceland, a diving and snorkeling trip to the Bahamas, and a diving trip to the Dry Tortugas, off the coast of Florida.

Membership Information and Volunteer Possibilities

Members can actively participate in the society through the regional offices and the affiliate. Members can take field trips, mostly on the East Coast, such as oyster dives, beach walks, whale watching, canoeing and rafting, diving trips, birding weekends, and camping trips. Annual membership is $20. Members receive the quarterly magazine *Underwater Naturalist*, a quarterly national newsletter the *Coastal Reporter*, and chapter newsletters and bulletins.

The Society's Divers' Section holds special events for underwater enthusiasts. Volunteers can participate in an annual fish tag-and-release program, which is designed to collect data for the National Marine Fisheries computer, in Massachusetts.

The society offers a wide range of activities to give members the opportunities to become actively involved with the environment. The opening of the office in Olympia, Washington makes activities readily available to members on both coasts.

☐ THE AMERICAN ORNITHOLOGISTS' UNION

Ornithological Societies of North America
P.O. Box 1897
Lawrence, KS 66044–8897
Contact: Stephen M. Russell, Secretary

History/Goals

The American Ornithologists' Union was founded in 1883 and is the oldest organization devoted to the scientific study of birds. AOU is primarily a professional organization, but its 4,000 members also include many amateurs with an interest in avian science.

AOU supports research on birds and undertakes projects on conservation issues. The primary activity of the American Ornithologists' Union is the publication of scientific information on birds.

Past Achievements

In 1983, AOU published *The Check-List of North American Birds*. This book is a detailed description of bird species and their distributions and habitats from the Arctic through Panama.

Ongoing Projects

AOU continues to fund scientific research and publishes reports of those studies and other important work in the field. *The Auk*, a quarterly journal of AOU, has been published for over 100 years and reports on original scientific research. *Ornithological Monographs* are an ongoing series of long research papers, published periodically since 1964.

Future Plans

Each year, AOU presents awards for excellence in research to individuals making significant achievements in the field of avian studies. The release of publications will continue to be the primary function of the American Ornithologists' Union.

Membership Information and Volunteer Possibilities

Regular annual membership in the union is $35. A life membership is available for $1,050. Members receive the quarterly journal, *The Auk*, a subscription to the bimonthly *Ornithological Newsletter*, and any supplements sent out during the year, as well as discounts on publications of the union.

An annual meeting provides members the chance to meet others with similar interests in birds. Participants attend lectures, films, workshops, exhibits, field trips, and social events. AOU members can also attend the quadrennial international congresses.

☐ AMERICAN RIVERS

801 Pennsylvania Avenue, SE, #303
Washington, DC 20003–2167
(202) 547-6900
Contacts: James M. Perry, Jr., Membership Director
Kevin Coyle, President

History/Goals

American Rivers was founded in 1973 to preserve America's rivers and surrounding landscapes. In the last half of the 1980s, American Rivers more than doubled its membership to over 14,000 members and quintupled its income to over $1.5 million annually.

American Rivers has a three-part goal: to add rivers to the Wild and Scenic Rivers System; to bring together local organizations, state and federal agencies, and private citizens in the interest of the nation's rivers;

and to help establish a new national energy policy to balance the needs to develop some rivers while preserving others.

Past Achievements

Since its founding, American Rivers helped preserve over 9,000 miles of American rivers, helped protect seven million acres of lands adjacent to protected rivers, stopped numerous ecologically destructive dams, and claims to have saved Americans over $23 billion in taxes.

Ongoing Projects

American Rivers' Public Lands Planning Program reviews all U.S. Forest Service and Bureau of Land Management plans to see that potential wild and scenic rivers are considered when determining land and water use on federal lands.

American Rivers works with the Forest Service and BLM to set up and implement directives for conducting river studies during the forest planning process.

Future Plans

American Rivers will continue to monitor all forest plans from the Forest Service and the BLM and will continue to make any necessary appeals to protect rivers they believe should be part of the Wild and Scenic Rivers System. American Rivers also plans to continue its involvement in workshops, festivals, river trips, and cleanups across the country.

Membership Information and Volunteer Possibilities

Individual membership in American Rivers is $20 annually, or $60 for a family. Members receive a subscription to the quarterly newsletter *American Rivers*, as well as action alerts and listings of river outfitters, fishing guides, canoe and kayak manufacturers, and retailers who support river conservation. Members are also eligible to apply for the American Rivers Card; a portion of each purchase made on this special MasterCard is contributed to American Rivers' projects.

Members close to the national office in Washington, D.C., are encouraged to volunteer in the office. American Rivers asks its national members to write to Congress, attend hearings, and work for river preservation at the local level. There are also internship programs available for college students and recent graduates.

☐ AMERICAN WILDLANDS

7500 E. Arapahoe Road, Suite 355
Englewood, CO 80112
(303) 771-0380
Contacts: Sally A. Ranney, President
Robin Brooksmith, Office Manager

History/Goals

In 1989, the American Wilderness Alliance became American Wildlands. The conservation organization was formed to protect and promote the proper management of America's publicly owned wildlands.

Past Achievements

In 1986 a timber management reform project was established to monitor existing timber management policies, challenge those practices damaging to wildlife and wildlands in the greater Yellowstone ecosystem, and suggest reforms to improve the system. One of the project's biggest victories was stopping the sale of 4.2 million board feet of timber near the Electric Peak Wilderness Area.

In 1987–88, AW helped a group of Colorado taxpayers create a network of people and organizations concerned with the political appointments of members to water conservancy boards.

Ongoing Projects

American Wildlands initiated a liaison project in 1989 for Dr. Richard Leakey, Kenya's Director of Wildlife Services. An American Wildlands/Leakey Elephant Fund has been established to assist in the project's efforts at gaining research and technical assistance and support here in the United States for Dr. Leakey's African programs.

AW has ongoing projects in New Mexico's Carrizo Mountains to protect the ancient juniper forests there. There is also an ongoing effort to persuade Congress to adopt a river legislation package to address key problems on America's river systems. The group works in Alaska to protect the caribou herd and its habitat from oil development.

In 1988 a watershed rehabilitation project was begun which will, over a five-year period, reintroduce beavers to New Mexico, Wyoming, and Colorado.

Future Plans

A major AW initiative entitled "Recreation-Conservation Connection" is aimed at the increasing number of people with an interest in outdoor recreation. By way of its newsletter and adventure programs, American Wildlands hopes to educate the public on how to enjoy the outdoors without destroying nature, as well as stimulate interest in the organization and its programs. The AW travel program has had as many as 600 participants in recent years and hopes to increase that number with the addition of trips to Rwanda, Patagonia, Antarctica, the Amazon, Belize, and the Alti region of the Soviet Union.

American Wildlands was successful in terminating a black bear hunt in Colorado in 1990 and plans to launch a similar program to stop the hunting of mountain lions in Colorado and to stop the use of hounds for hunting.

Membership Information & Volunteer Possibilities

American Wildlands has approximately 3,550 members. Regular membership dues are $22 annually, and members receive the annual magazine *Wild America*, the AW newsletter, legislative alerts, discounts on books and other items, and a guide to American Wildlands' wilderness trips.

The biggest opportunity to participate within this organization is through the more than eighty wilderness trips offered each year.

☐ ANIMAL LEGAL DEFENSE FUND
1363 Lincoln Avenue
San Rafael, CA 94901
(415) 459-0885
Contact: Joyce Tischler, Executive Director

History/Goals
The Animal Legal Defense Fund was founded in 1979 as Attorneys for Animal Rights. The name was changed in 1984, and today the group is often called "the law firm of the animal rights movement." There are currently 250 attorney members and over 40,000 supporting members in the organization, and there are seven local groups. ALDF deals with issues affecting animals, hunting, trapping, international wildlife, and endangered species. The group's work is done through litigation.

Past Achievements
During 1988 and 1989 ALDF worked through the courts to halt the hunting of mountain lions in California and to stop the annual deer hunt in Illinois. Also during 1989 ALDF won a victory in the California courts when the annual California black bear hunt was canceled through a court decision.

ALDF was successful during 1989 in getting the U.S. Department of Agriculture to release regulations on the treatment of animals used in laboratory research.

Ongoing Projects
The Animal Legal Defense Fund provides legal services as necessary in the fight for animal welfare. ALDF works to convince the state fish and game departments that their purpose is to protect wildlife rather than uphold hunting interests.

During 1989 ALDF began a nationwide toll-free hotline service. This service is designed to provide advice and legal support for students opposing animal dissection in the classroom.

Future Plans
ALDF plans to continue to work through the courts to fight for animal rights. ALDF plans to continue protecting and to expand the legal rights of animals throughout the 1990s.

Membership Information and Volunteer Possibilities
Annual membership in the Animal Legal Defense Fund is $15. Members receive a free subscription to the quarterly magazine, *The Animals' Advocate.*

ALDF encourages members to write letters and sign petitions for legislative action. Members are also encouraged to work for animal rights at the local level.

☐ ANIMAL PROTECTION INSTITUTE OF AMERICA
2831 Fruitridge Road
P.O. Box 22505
Sacramento, CA 95822
(916) 731-5521
Contacts: Duf Fischer, Executive Director
Nancy Crooks, General Manager
Emily Baker, Librarian

History/Goals
Animal Protection Institute was founded in 1968 to educate the public and someday alleviate cruelty to animals, the overpopulation of unwanted pets, and the abandonment and neglect of animals. API also works to preserve natural animal habitats and protect the animals in those habitats.

API today has over 150,000 members and is involved in issues such as wild horse roundups, fur wearing, the use of animals for testing, factory farming, marine mammals captured for aquariums, and dolphin and whale killing.

Past Achievements
In the late 1980s API, together with Fund for Animals, won a case that outlawed the mass adoption of wild horses. This court battle resulted in a 10 to 20 percent reduction in the number of horses seized annually.

In 1989 API had over 2,500 volunteers working on its Trap Force. These volunteers brought the issue of fur wearing to the public's attention and succeeded in bringing out the horror stories told by the trappers themselves.

Ongoing Projects
One of API's biggest ongoing projects is the API library, under the supervision of librarian Emily Baker. The expanding library receives over 4,000 requests for information annually from students, teachers, researchers, and writers. The library includes species files, government publications, information from other organizations and individuals, along with 3,600 magazines and 2,500 books.

One of API's major campaigns is Pet Watch, envisioned as a national identification system that API hopes to implement to track down stolen animals. It will use a tattoo identification on the animal and the national identification system already in place that is used by law enforcement offices to track down stolen merchandise.

A division was established in the Animal Protection Institute in 1989 to bring reform to factory-style farming in the United States. Through public awareness campaigns, API hopes to bring the industry to its knees.

Future Plans

Animal Protection Institute is taking the lead to stop marine mammal captivity. API hopes to make the public aware of the severely shortened lifespans of captive marine mammals and eventually prevent the capture of animals used in attractions at aquariums.

API is working to block the importation of wild-caught birds into the United States, citing as evidence the statistics that only one of approximately every nine birds captured survives; the other eight die in transit.

Membership Information and Volunteer Possibilities

Animal Protection Institute is a grassroots organization that depends largely on volunteers across the country. Annual membership, which includes a subscription to the quarterly magazine *Mainstream* plus posters, publications, and reports, is $20.

Volunteer possibilities within the organization are nearly limitless. Currently over 10,000 API members are actively involved on task forces. The general API Emergency Force has nearly 7,000 members, and there are more specialized task forces such as the Trap Force. The Act Force is a network of people involved in individual issues at the local level, who can obtain counsel and coordination from the national staff.

Animal Protection Institute is a storehouse of information for researchers, educators, and teachers. In addition to the API library, there is a constant outpouring of humane-education informational materials. There are also periodic newsletters, which provide specific information and recommendations. *A.P.E. Vine* is a special newsletter targeted toward teachers and classrooms.

☐ THE ANTARCTICA PROJECT

218 D Street, SE
Washington, DC 20003
(202) 544-2600
Contact: Elizabeth Schandelmeier, Executive Assistant

History/Goals

The Antarctica Project was founded in 1982 to protect Antarctica. The project monitors the region and lobbies at both the national and international levels.

The Antarctica Project monitors ongoing negotiations and important political meetings. The project is a member of the Antarctic and Southern Ocean Coalition (ASOC). ASOC has 200 member organizations from thirty-five countries.

Past Achievements

The Antarctica Project served as an expert adviser during 1989 to the U.S. Office of Technology Assessment on its study and report of the Minerals Convention.

The project wrote a study paper outlining the need for a comprehensive environmental protection convention.

A conservation strategy on Antarctica was developed with the International Union for Conservation of Nature and Natural Resources.

Ongoing Projects

The Antarctica Project conducts policy research and legal analysis. The group presents testimony and policy proposals to Congress and other government agencies.

The Antarctica Project has an extensive list of publications, including articles, books, videos, and posters, for all ages. The project serves as a clearinghouse of information for the public.

In 1988 ASOC received a limited observer status to the Convention on the Conservation of Antarctic Marine Living Resources (CCAMLR). So far, the observer status continues to be renewed, providing ASOC with a way to monitor CCAMLR and to present proposals.

Future Plans

Besides continuing on with the work it has already begun, the Antarctica Project has several new goals. The project is calling for the designation of Antarctica as a world park.

The Antarctica Project is working on a bilateral plan to pump out the oil and salvage the *Bahia Paraiso*, which sank in early 1989 near the U.S. Palmer Station. The salvage cost is estimated at $50 million.

Membership Information and Volunteer Possibilities

Annual membership in the Antarctica Project is $30; a family can join for $40. Members receive a copy of *ECO*, the international paper produced by ASOC.

☐ APPALACHIAN TRAIL CONFERENCE

Washington & Jackson Streets
P.O. Box 807
Harpers Ferry, WV 25425
(304) 535-6331
Contact: David N. Startzell, Executive Director

History/Goals

The Appalachian Trail Conference was founded by Benton MacKaye on March 3, 1925, to coordinate the building of the trail by club volunteers. Mr. MacKaye, who originally proposed the trail concept, was assisted by leaders of eastern trail organizations, officials of the National Park Service and the U.S. Forest Service, and forest and park superintendents. Today the purpose of the ATC is to protect the 2,135 miles of trail from Georgia to Maine and to manage the thousands of acres of publicly owned land serving as a buffer for the Trail.

The conference, headquartered in Harpers Ferry, West Virginia, has four field offices and over 20,000 individual members. The trail is maintained by over 4,000 volunteers working through thirty-one organizations that cooperate with ATC.

The Appalachian Trail was designated the first national scenic trail in 1968, and funds were appropriated to acquire surrounding land as a buffer zone. The Appalachian Trail crosses eight national forests, six parcels of the national park system, sixty state parks and game preserves, and numerous small communities.

Past Achievements

In 1968 the National Trails System Act was signed into law. This act protects the trail and gives the U.S. Department of the Interior, National Park Service, the primary responsibility for upkeep of the trail. However, because of ATC's more than thirty years of dedication to the trail, the Interior Department gave back to it the responsibility of ensuring the protection of the trail.

Ongoing Projects

The Appalachian Trail Conference has a number of programs to protect, manage, and promote the Appalachian Trail. The conference briefs Congress on land-acquisition problems, conducts field studies and corridor designs, and monitors abuses of the trail. The conference determines all maintenance requirements for the trail and sponsors workshops, publishes manuals, and establishes work crews.

ATC produces a number of guidebooks and maps of the trail, as well as natural history books on surrounding areas. It maintains an archive and a visitors' center at the headquarters.

Future Plans

The ATC plans to keep promoting and protecting the Appalachian Trail. Some of the trail still passes through private land, and the conference is working to purchase all such land, in addition to acquiring more buffer land to hold back encroaching development.

Membership Information and Volunteer Possibilities

Annual membership in the Appalachian Trail Conference is $25, or $18 if you already belong to a maintaining club cooperating with ATC on the trail. There is a family membership for $30 and a student/senior membership for $18. Members receive discounts on maps, guidebooks, and other publications, as well as a discount on lodging at northern Virginia's Bears Den hostel. Members also receive a subscription to the organization's magazine, *Appalachian Trailway News*, and a 120-page handbook on ATC history, programs, and volunteer opportunities.

The biggest involvement in ATC is through actual trail use, either as a volunteer worker or an outdoor enthusiast. Nearly two-thirds of the U.S. population lives within a day's drive of some portion of the Appalachian Trail, making it easy to take advantage of this scenic footpath.

☐ AUDUBON NATURALIST SOCIETY OF THE CENTRAL ATLANTIC STATES

8940 Jones Mill Road
Chevy Chase, MD 20815
(301) 652-9188
Contacts: Ken Nicholls, Executive Director
Cris Fleming, Education Director

History/Goals

The Audubon Naturalist Society (not affiliated with the National Audubon Society) was founded in 1897 and is one of the oldest of the independent Audubon societies. The goal of ANS is to "increase public awareness of the natural environment and to encourage participation in efforts to preserve and renew our natural resources." The two major areas of work at the society are in educational programs and an active conservation program.

The Audubon Naturalist Society is headquartered at Woodend, a forty-acre wildlife preserve in Chevy Chase, Maryland.

Past Achievements

The Audubon Naturalist Society has always made the preservation of natural areas a priority. Over thirty years ago society members, including Justice William O. Douglas, helped to preserve the C&O Canal in Washington, D.C., as national parkland.

Ongoing Projects

Carrying on the message of former member Rachel Carson's *Silent Spring*, the society currently works to prevent the use of herbicides in the Potomac River that poison birds and their habitats and works to keep homeowners informed about the uses and misuses of pesticides.

Audubon Naturalist Society has several ongoing, long-term monitoring projects, such as bald eagle surveys, breeding bird censuses, and Christmas counts.

The society sponsors over 100 field trips annually to natural areas from Dyke Marsh just out of Washington, D.C., to the Great Smoky Mountains. Nature classes for children over the age of four and family programs are carried out throughout the year. Audubon Lectures host a scientist at the Smithsonian Museum of Natural History each month. Environmental education workshops are held throughout the year to give the necessary environmental training to teachers and youth leaders.

The society offers a complete curriculum of courses, the Natural History Field Studies program, through the USDA Graduate School, a certificate program located in Washington, D.C.

Future Plans

The Audubon Naturalist Society will continue to sponsor lectures, seminars, workshops, and other informational programs that serve to educate the public. The society will also continue to sponsor field trips, to help in the efforts to protect natural areas, and to bring as much information about the environment as possible to the public.

Membership Information and Volunteer Possibilities

Annual membership in the Audubon Naturalist Society of the Central Atlantic States is $25 for an individual, $35 for a family. There are reduced memberships available for seniors and students. Members receive *Audubon Naturalist News* and society publications printed throughout the year. Members are also eligible for the environmental education programs at special member prices, can attend Audubon Lectures at the Smithsonian Museum of Natural History at discount rates, receive a 10 percent discount at Audubon Naturalist Bookshops in the Washington, D.C., area, and receive invitations to special programs and exhibits at Woodend. The society also sponsors hundreds of field trips each year, which are free of charge to members.

Volunteers are frequently utilized in the society. Volunteers work at Woodend and in the society bookshops, run the speakers bureau, lead field trips, organize special events, and teach in the school ecology project in District of Columbia public schools. Volunteers are used extensively in the summer children's programs. These volunteers are generally high school students, who work in conjunction with interns and teachers.

☐ BAT CONSERVATION INTERNATIONAL

P.O. Box 162603
Austin, TX 78716–2603
(512) 327-9721
Contact: Dr. Merlin D. Tuttle, Executive Director

History/Goals

Bat Conservation International was formed in 1982 by Dr. Merlin Tuttle, biologist and conservationist. The organization was developed to promote, through public education and conservation practices, the protection of bats and their habitat. BCI today has over 8,000 members from 54 countries and is recognized as the international leader in bat conservation. BCI is the international resource center for bat information. A scientific staff conducts research and adds to the data base of pertinent information. BCI helps countries worldwide conduct regional education programs.

Past Achievements

BCI helped create a seventy-six-square-mile national park in American Samoa to protect the habitats for Samoan and Tongan flying foxes. This tropical rain forest, home to a number of other plants and animals found nowhere else in the world, is the first rain forest to be protected by the U.S. National Park Service.

In 1988 BCI hired its first education director, to enable the group to focus on educational outreach programs.

Dr. Tuttle published *America's Neighborhood Bats* in 1988 with the University of Texas Press; it is a comprehensive guide to North American bats.

Ongoing Projects

In 1989 BCI began a long-term study on the role of bats in the pollination of saguaro, cardon, and organ pipe cacti in the Sonoran Desert. The project was funded by a grant from the National Geographic Society.

BCI receives hundreds of requests each year for educational materials on bats. In response to this demand, the "Bats of America" audiovisual program was developed. The fifteen-minute program is used by schools, nature centers, zoos, libraries, museums, parks, and many other groups and institutions.

Future Plans

BCI plans to continue public education and scientific research in an effort to encourage conservation activities for and an understanding of this member of the mammal population.

Membership Information and Volunteer Possibilities

Annual membership in Bat Conservation International is $25, and there are student and senior discounts. Members receive the quarterly magazine, *BATS*, as well as discounts on items in the gift catalog.

Volunteers are occasionally used in fieldwork or to help out in the organization offices.

☐ THE BROOKS BIRD CLUB

707 Warwood Avenue
Wheeling, West Virginia 26003
(304) 547-5253
Contact: Helen Conrad, Administrator

History/Goals

The Brooks Bird Club was founded in 1932 by John W. Handlan and a group of outdoor enthusiasts who took weekly bird walks together. A. B. Brooks, a West Virginia naturalist, often accompanied the group, and when the new organization was formed, it was named after this well-respected and influential man.

The club's major purpose is to promote the study and enjoyment of birds and the rest of the natural world. The club informs members on environmental issues and encourages preservation and conservation. There are currently more than 1,000 members from thirty-eight states in the United States and eleven foreign countries.

Past Achievements

Dr. George A. Hall, a club member, published a hardcover reference book, *Birds of West Virginia,* and the club also published *The List of West Virginia Birds* by Dr. Hall in 1971.

A "Field Check List of Birds" was printed by BBC and is widely used by members to record their sightings.

Ongoing Projects

Annually in June a foray is held in a region of West Virginia. Members in the field participate in an ecological study of that year's area. The week is spent birding, studying plants, and attending field trips, and evenings are used for films, slide shows, and guest speakers.

Ongoing projects include bird population studies, creating slide shows for groups, acquiring land, surveying breeding birds, annual hawk counts, winter bird feeder counts, bird banding, and the West Virginia Breeding Bird Atlas Project, which receives financial support from the Non-Game Wildlife Fund of the West Virginia Department of Natural Resources. The club serves as a clearinghouse for the general public and has a library with over 750 volumes pertaining to birds and other aspects of natural history.

Future Plans

Most of BBC's projects are annual and will continue into the future. A waterfowl field trip to Seneca Lake, Ohio, is planned each spring. An eastern shore waterfowl trip takes place each November. Activities are planned nearly every month for members.

Membership Information and Volunteer Possibilities

Annual individual memberships in the Brooks Bird Club are $14. Families can join for $17 and students for $5. A lifetime membership can be obtained for $200.

Along with participating in the annual foray and other activities and outings of the group, members receive the BBC publications. *The Redstart* is the official publication of the Brooks Bird Club. Published quarterly since 1933, the magazine includes original natural history papers. *The Mail Bag* is the quarterly newsletter, begun in 1942.

☐ CALIFORNIA MARINE MAMMAL CENTER

Marin Headlands
Golden Gate National Recreation Area
Sausalito, CA 94965
(415) 331-SEAL
Contacts: Denize Springer, Development and
                Communications
             Peigin Barrett, Executive Director

History/Goals

The California Marine Mammal Center was founded in 1975 to rescue and rehabilitate sick, injured, or distressed marine mammals. CMMC is licensed by the federal government to handle marine mammals and is supported by members worldwide.

The center was established on an abandoned Nike missile base in the Golden Gate National Recreation Area, across the bay from San Francisco. The center occupies a seven-acre site under a permit from the National Park Service. The work of the California Marine Mammal Center is carred out by over 300 volunteers, whose work is overseen by a team of animal care professionals.

Past Achievements

Since its founding in 1975, CMMC has saved hundreds of marine mammals, such as Behemoth, an orphaned elephant seal pup. When CMMC found Behemoth, he was blind, sick, and starving, stranded on a California beach. CMMC rescued the pup, performed a three-hour cataract surgery (the first ever on his species), nursed him until he'd reached 200 pounds, and released him back into the ocean.

The center has also provided valuable resource data to various scientific and veterinary institutions around the world, collected in its work to save and rehabilitate the marine mammals.

During fall 1989, CMMC was the featured organization in a one-hour special entitled "Conserving America." The special was aired by Pittsburgh's PBS station, WQED, and focused on conservation along America's coastlines. The center has also won numerous awards, including the President's Volunteer Action Award in 1989, the Chevron Conservation Award in 1987, and the JC Penney Golden Rule Award for Volunteerism in 1987.

Ongoing Projects

The California Marine Mammal Center has an ongoing rescue program along the Pacific Coast from San Luis Obispo, California, to the Oregon border. The center works with sea lions, northern elephant seals, harbor seals, norther fur seals, norther or Steller sea lions, Guadalupe fur seals, common dolphins, harbor porpoises, gray whales, and killer whales. Rehabilitation of an injured animal usually takes anywhere from three to eight months or longer.

CMMC has an active education department that works to make the public more aware of the ocean's ecosystem and the marine environment. The center is open to the public every day of the year from 10:00 A.M. to 4:00 P.M. and provides an up-close look at CMMC's operations. Nearly 60,000 people visit the center each year. Its hands-on programs provide excellent training for school children.

Future Plans

The center's plans for the five-year period 1990 to 1995 include expanding the animal care pen and the microbiology lab, constructing a cetacean rehabilitation pool, and constructing an environmental education center.

Membership Information and Volunteer Possibilities

Annual membership in the center is $18 and includes a subscription to the quarterly publication *CMMC News*. Members also receive a 10 percent discount on items in the gift shop as well as invitations to special events, behind-the-scenes tours, lectures, and nature expeditions.

Members can participate in CMMC's annual wildlife journeys, which explore the Maine coast from a 125-foot schooner. There is also an educational program available for grades K through 6. The program includes background information, lesson plans, activities, puzzles, and other information. The guide is available for $6.

Volunteers account for approximately 95 percent of CMMC's work-force. There are currently over 300 volunteers in the organization who each devote between forty and sixty hours each month to the program. Volunteers drive along the California coast watching for animals in trouble; they work with the medical teams to nurse sick and injured animals back to health. Volunteers also do a variety of other jobs at the center, including staffing the gift shop and information booth, maintaining the facilities and equipment, assisting in data processing and membership work, and handling public relations.

☐ CARIBBEAN CONSERVATION CORPORATION

P.O. Box 2866
Gainesville, FL 32602
(904) 373-6441
Contacts: David Carr, Executive Director
Lynne A. Warren, Office Manager

History/Goals
The Caribbean Conservation Corporation was founded in 1954 by a group of conservationists inspired by Florida zoologist Archie Carr's book, *The Windward Road,* which brought to life the plight of the green turtle. The focus of CCC is on the seasonal monitoring of the western Caribbean green turtle colony at Tortuguero, Costa Rica. CCC also supports and participates in other conservation projects throughout the world. Dr. Archie Carr was the technical director of CCC and directed all research until his death in 1987.

Past Achievements
Caribbean Conservation Corporation was instrumental in getting a twenty-mile-long stretch of beach in Costa Rica designated a turtle sanctuary and in establishing the Tortuguero National Park.

During the 1960s CCC, with the help of the U.S. Navy, released over 100,000 Tortuguero turtle hatchlings on beaches throughout the Caribbean, the Bahamas, Florida, and Bermuda as part of Operation Green Turtle. The hatchlings were released in areas where the turtles were once native but had been wiped out by humans.

Ongoing Projects
Every summer since its establishment in 1954, teams of students work at the research station at Tortuguero, tagging and recording the arrivals of

female green turtles that lay their eggs on the beach. Over 20,000 turtles have been tagged during the program's existence.

CCC's Adopt-a-Turtle campaign, in a combined effort with the Nestle Food Corporation, works to save the species from extinction. A pamphlet explaining the program has been packaged with Nestle's DeMet's Turtles candy. The program is trying to educate the public about the endangered turtles and is attempting to generate financial support for the continuation of conservation programs. In the first eight months of the project, over 4,000 sea turtles were "adopted" for a $15 donation. DeMet's established a "Save the Turtles Fund" with an initial $50,000 donation to thirteen individual sea turtle organizations, including CCC.

Future Plans
CCC has proposed a national wildlife refuge on a 20.5-mile stretch of the Florida coast. The area, nesting site for approximately 10,000 to 12,000 turtles annually, is to be named after Dr. Archie Carr.

Caribbean Conservation Corporation plans to continue the program of tagging turtles at Tortuguero. The information is used to add to CCC's data base. CCC also plans to establish sanctuaries and preserves in the western Caribbean and to fully expand its work into that area of the Caribbean.

Membership Information and Volunteer Possibilities
Annual membership in Caribbean Conservation Corporation is $35 for an individual or $50 for a family. Membership includes a subscription to the quarterly newsletter, *Velador*.

The Sea Turtle Research program at Tortuguero, Costa Rica, and the annual tagging at the research station in Tortuguero are volunteer programs. Each year volunteers from a variety of backgrounds assist scientists in studying and reporting on the turtles at Tortuguero. Volunteers depart Miami for either a ten-day or a seventeen-day program. The programs, coordinated by the Massachusetts Audubon Society, cost between $1,422 and $1,971 per person, depending on the program chosen, and include airfare, meals, and accommodations.

☐ CENTER FOR HOLISTIC RESOURCE MANAGEMENT

800 Rio Grande Boulevard, NW, Suite 10
Albuquerque, NM 87104
(505) 242-9272
Contacts: Hal Norris, Chief Executive Officer
Jeanne Fernandez, Administrative Assistant

History/Goals
The Center for Holistic Resource Management was formed in 1984 by African-born ecologist Allan Savory. It was developed as an alternative to conventional resource management approaches, and is a nonpolitical

organization that works to make the public more aware of holistic management. The major focus of the center is on education. Savory's holistic model, which can be utilized to solve management problems at all levels, takes the complexities of our ecosystem into account. The model is now used by ranchers and farmers, policy makers, researchers, and small business owners.

The organization today consists of ranchers, farmers, wildlifers, foresters, researchers, educators, conservationists, and consultants from across the country. There are affiliate branches in New Mexico, Nebraska, Arizona, Colorado, Oregon/Washington/Idaho, Montana, North Dakota, Texas/Oklahoma, Canada, Mexico, and Namibia. The board of directors consists of representatives from diverse areas and includes ranchers, farmers, environmentalists, educators, scientists, and members at large.

The center has a long list of goals that it strives to meet through its programs: to produce stable environments with sound watersheds; to restore profitability to agricultural operations; to improve water resources of urban areas as well as industry and agriculture; to increase wildlife species; to restore the stability of streamside areas; to prevent the waste of financial resources through poor management techniques; and to increase citizen participation.

Past Achievements

The major function of the organization is to provide education. The center has developed eleven different courses ranging from "Restoring the Land While Increasing Profits and Enhancing Productivity" to "Generating Wealth: Planning Your Financial Success," "Biological Planning and Monitoring," "New Ideas for Sustaining Farm Profits," and "Enriching Relationships for Couples: A Retreat for New Growth."

In 1990 Allan Savory published *Holistic Resource Management,* which outlines his model of holistic land management.

Ongoing Projects

The center currently sponsors its eleven courses at twenty different locations throughout the United States and Canada. The HRM Degree Program offers continuing education credits for courses taken.

An annual meeting each February offers members the chance to network with other members from across the country. There are guest speakers, workshops, and the chance to meet with international members and representatives.

Future Plans

The Center for Holistic Resource Management plans to increase its member base and establish training centers throughout the critical areas of the world, specifically in Latin America, Africa, Asia, and Australia. The center plans to have a multilingual staff to operate the centers around the world.

The center plans to increase its public awareness program, and there are plans over the next few years for a national television special. The center also plans to develop self-guiding educational materials that can be utilized by schoolchildren as well as conservationists and policy makers. The center also seeks to have courses on holistic management accepted and integrated into the curriculum of various schools and universities.

The center plans to put together a scientific team of representatives from the center, universities, and the private and public sector to monitor the applications of the center's methods. The center also plans to work with other organizations having similar interests and goals, and would like to work on the formation of coalitions.

Membership Information and Volunteer Possibilities
Annual membership is $35 for individuals. There is a reduced membership of $20 available to students and seniors. Family businesses can join for $50 and organizations for $100. Members receive a one-year subscription to *The HRM Newsletter*, plus a membership in an affiliate branch, updates on courses and the degree program, discounts on all HRM products, and an invitation to the annual meeting.

The local affiliates are the grass roots portion of the organization. Members can become involved at the local level through education and through actual applications of the HRM methods.

☐ CENTER FOR MARINE CONSERVATION
1725 DeSales Street, NW
Washington, DC 20036
(202) 429-5609
Contact: Donna Brass, Director of Membership

History/Goals
The Center for Marine Conservation was founded in 1972 to help protect marine wildlife and their habitats. The center currently has over 110,000 members, a home office in Washington, D.C., and offices in Texas, California, Virginia, and Florida. The center has four major goals: conserving marine habitats; preventing marine pollution; managing fisheries for conservation; and protecting endangered marine species. The center meets these goals through research, public education, citizen involvement, and by supporting conservation programs.

Past Achievements
In 1986 CMC helped establish the world's first whale sanctuary, the Silver Bank Humpback Whale Sanctuary near the Dominican Republic.

In 1988 the center established a data base on marine debris. This one-of-a-kind data base was compiled and analyzed by the center to help researchers attempting to understand specific debris problems and work out solutions.

The center has funded educational materials that are used in Latin America and the Caribbean. CMC also published the *Citizen's Guide to Plastic in the Ocean: More Than a Litter Problem* in 1988 to be used as a handbook for policy makers and the concerned public.

Since 1981 the Marine Habitat Program of CMC has helped secure six new national marine sanctuaries in the United States.

Ongoing Projects

In 1987 the Center began a joint program with the National Oceanic and Atmospheric Administration (NOAA) and the Society of the Plastics Industry aimed at educating the merchant shipping, commercial fishing, and plastics manufacturing industries about the hazards of marine debris. The project has been expanded to include recreational fishermen and boaters.

The center has been working with several organizations concerning the conservation of sea turtles. There is an ongoing project with the U.S. Fish and Wildlife Service in Florida to help protect Florida's sea turtles from the effects of beachfront lighting that adversely affect the nesting turtles.

The center sponsors annual coastal cleanups, which help illustrate the problem of marine debris.

The center has established two Marine Debris Information offices, one in Washington, D.C., to serve the Atlantic and Gulf of Mexico regions and one in San Francisco to serve the Pacific region. These offices send out information on marine debris to scientists, policy makers, educators, and the general public.

Future Plans

The Center for Marine Conservation plans to continue its programs aimed at protecting marine wildlife. CMC works to educate the public about the hazards of nylon fishing nets, plastics, and other marine debris. The species recovery program works to conserve endangered species. The organization encourages the designation of marine sanctuaries and encourages the public to become involved in the preservation of marine life and marine habitat.

Membership Information and Volunteer Possibilities

Basic membership in the Center for Marine Conservation is $20 annually. Members receive a subscription to *Marine Conservation News*, the quarterly newsletter; action alerts; and discounts on merchandise in the Whale Gifts catalog. The center also publishes the *Entanglement Network Newsletter* to keep members up-to-date on marine entanglement in debris.

Members are encouraged to volunteer their time to become actively involved in the center. Members are asked to write to Congress in support of marine conservation. Every year, volunteers participate in the beach cleanups sponsored by the center in various parts of the country. In 1988, for example, over 16,000 people participated in the cleanups in Texas and Florida.

☐ CENTER FOR PLANT CONSERVATION
125 Arborway
Jamaica Plain, MA 02130–3520
(617) 524-6988
Contact: Donald A. Falk, Executive Director

History/Goals
The Center for Plant Conservation was established in 1984 for the conservation and study of endangered plants native to the United States. The center created the National Collection of Endangered Plants, a living collection of endangered plant species. The collection is distributed among more than twenty botanic gardens across the United States. The plant collections are supplemented by a seed bank administered by the National Plant Germplasm System of the U.S. Department of Agriculture. Coordination and support of the program are provided from the national office in Massachusetts, while the program is executed at the various regional gardens.

The center's major goals are to maintain the National Collection of Endangered Plants and associated programs and educational programs; to develop and maintain an accessible data base of endangered plants in the United States; to work on conservation projects in conjunction with other organizations; to assist botanic gardens throughout the United States in establishing endangered plant programs; and to develop research programs exploring endangered native plants.

Past Achievements
Since its founding, the Center for Plant Conservation has brought over 300 different kinds of rare and endangered plants into its program. These species are now being cultivated in the botanic gardens or are in seed storage.

Ongoing Projects
The center works with local, national, and international organizations to study horticultural practices and botanical collections. CPC also studies rare plant distribution. The center has established and is constantly expanding a computerized data base, which is available to conservation agencies, natural resource managers, horticulturists, and scientists.

Future Plans
In early 1990 CPC and the Bureau of Land Management signed an agreement in which CPC and BLM will work together to manage and recover rare and endangered plants on federal lands. CPC will work with

BLM state offices to develop projects to be carried out over several years. These projects will include such things as plant reintroduction, off-site plant and seed storage, conservation research, and the training of BLM personnel in the implementation of conservation techniques involving the plants.

Membership Information and Volunteer Information

Annual membership in the Center for Plant Conservation, which includes a subscription to the quarterly report, *Plant Conservation*, is a minimum of $35.

For those wishing to become more involved in the organization, there is an intern program as well as a public education program. The center suggests that members sponsor a species in the National Collection of Endangered Plants. A contribution of $5,000 is matched by an endowment from the Andrew W. Mellon Foundation and will set up a "trust fund" for the species.

☐ CITIZENS' CLEARINGHOUSE FOR HAZARDOUS WASTES

Box 926
Arlington, VA 22216
(703) 276-7070
Contact: Lois Marie Gibbs, Executive Director

History/Goals

Citizens' Clearinghouse for Hazardous Wastes was founded in 1981 by Lois Marie Gibbs, former Love Canal leader. CCHW serves as a service center for the Grassroots Movement for Environmental Justice and aids individuals trying to form new groups as well as established grassroots groups needing assistance. CCHW focuses on hazardous wastes, solid waste, industrial discharges, medical waste, workplace exposure, industrial accidents, radioactive waste, sewage sludge, household toxics, asbestos, and the release of any other substances threatening environmental justice. CCHW does not lobby or file lawsuits on behalf of the Grassroots Movement but helps the local groups take action for themselves.

Past Achievements

CCHW has grown from a staff of two volunteers in Lois Gibbs's basement to a paid staff of fourteen. Besides the offices in Arlington there are offices in Alabama, California, Pennsylvania, Texas, Ohio, and Virginia serving over 7,000 members nationwide.

CCHW has helped numerous small, mostly rural citizen groups prevent the creation of dumps and incinerators. CCHW teaches them such skills as organizing, research, and media relations, enabling them to fight the battle themselves. Through CCHW's efforts, over 400 waste sites were blocked throughout the country between 1987 and 1990.

Ongoing Projects

Every three years CCHW hosts a Grassroots Convention, allowing grassroots leaders from all over the world to come together to exchange ideas and develop new policies. In the interim, CCHW hosts roundtables and conferences for grassroots organizations.

CCHW helps local groups establish strategy, begin fund-raising, and conduct background research. CCHW also provides resource materials, training, and networking among groups. CCHW also answers many questions from individuals, such as health questions, questions on chemical exposure, legal issues, and safe alternatives.

CCHW gives on-site assistance to various groups throughout the country. During these road visits, CCHW representatives provide help in planning strategy, help with local fund-raising projects, and speak at rallies, workshops, or other media events.

CCHW provides technical assistance to individuals and groups. This technical assistance may be in the form of interpreting volumes of technical reports or in issuing simple one-page fact sheets in clear, understandable language. CCHW also publishes a large number of guidebooks and other sources on environmental issues. The group also has an extensive library on waste topics.

CCHW maintains files on major corporate polluters in the United States. Grassroots activists can get information to help them prepare profiles and to help them narrow their research.

Future Plans

CCHW, through the Grassroots Movement, hopes to someday end all unsafe disposal practices and to implement mandatory use of safe alternatives. CCHW will not compromise with polluters on issues affecting the life and health of human beings. CCHW plans to continue working to provide the necessary information to individuals and groups trying to combat the spread of toxic wastes.

Membership Information and Volunteer Possibilities

Annual membership in the Citizens' Clearinghouse for Hazardous Wastes is $25 for individuals, $35 for community groups, and $15 for students and seniors. Members receive a subscription to the bimonthly magazine *Everyone's Backyard*, along with discounts on T-shirts, publications, training conferences, and water and radon test kits.

Volunteer opportunities are available at the local level, and a network of volunteer correspondents throughout the United States keep CCHW informed of events across the country.

☐ THE COASTAL SOCIETY

5410 Grosvenor Lane, Suite 110
Bethesda, MD 20814
(301) 897-8616
Contact: Thomas E. Bigford, Executive Director

History/Goals
The Coastal Society was established in 1975 to improve interdisciplinary cooperation and communication among professionals, public interest groups, and private citizens; to effectively promote the wise use of coastal resources; and to increase public knowledge, understanding, and appreciation of coastal areas.

Past Achievements
The Coastal Society has sponsored numerous conferences in which participants from varied disciplines have confronted coastal problems. Past conferences included "The Present and Future of Coasts," "Energy Across the Coastal Zone," "Resource Allocation Issues in the Coastal Environment," "Communicating Coastal Information," and "Gambling with the Shore."

Ongoing Projects
The society sponsors workshops throughout the United States in conjunction with government agencies, academic institutions, private organizations, and professional groups. A number of items are published each year, including the proceedings of the annual meetings.

The Coastal Society develops congressional testimony on coastal management, conservation, and water quality. Special planning assistance is available to organizations and government agencies interested in coastal management in Latin America.

Future Plans
The Coastal Society is drafting a statement of policy and plans to take public positions on proposed policies affecting coastal issues. The society will continue to endorse and sponsor meetings, conferences, and workshops, and plans to work on developing international ties.

Membership Information and Volunteer Possibilities
Annual membership in The Coastal Society is $25 within the United States. Reduced memberships are available for students, and special memberships are available for libraries and institutions. Members receive a subscription to the quarterly publication, The Coastal Society *Bulletin*.

☐ CONSERVATION INTERNATIONAL

1015 18th Street, NW, Suite 1000
Washington, DC 20036
(202) 429-5660
Contact: Amina Khaalis, Membership Services

History/Goals
Conservation International was organized in 1987, when it split off from Nature Conservancy. CI today has an annual budget of $4.6 million and over 55,000 members. The organization is currently headed by Russell Mittermeier, who left World Wildlife Fund in 1989. Mittermeier is a primatologist and remains an active field scientist.

CI has four major themes: focusing on entire ecosystems; integrating economic interests with ecological interests; creating a base of scientific knowledge necessary to make conservation-minded decisions; and making it possible for conservation to be understood and implemented at the local level.

Rather than going into other nations around the world and attempting to carry out conservation practices for the local people, Conservation International acts as a catalyst for conservation. CI works with local people and governments, ensuring that the people affected by conservation practices will have a say in the implementation and will reap the benefits of the programs.

CI works in countries throughout Latin America and the Caribbean, including Bolivia, Costa Rica, Mexico, Guatemala, and Peru.

Conservation International's board of directors and worldwide staff is composed of nationals from the countries in which the program exists.

Past Achievements
Conservation International was the originator of the debt-for-nature swaps, which have proven successful during the organization's first few years of operation. In 1988 swaps were concluded in Bolivia and Costa Rica that totaled approximately $750,000. In Costa Rica CI helped the local government establish a natural resources conservation fund, used to convert $5.4 million of bank debt into local currency bonds.

To build an effective local knowledge base, CI has helped develop conservation data centers (CDCs) throughout Latin America and the Caribbean and currently has eight such centers.

In February 1989 CI held the first training course for forestry service personnel in Bolivia. In Mexico in 1989, biologists from the Institute of Biology at the University of Mexico, with CI support, completed preliminary field research on critical island areas in the Sea of Cortes, which will be used to help create an information base. Also in Mexico, the country's first nonprofit conservation organization, FUNDAMAT, was formed with CI's support in 1989.

A software package was completed in 1988 to provide much-needed mapping technology to Latin American institutions at no charge. A map data base completed in 1989 can be updated regularly and linked to statistical data bases.

Ongoing Projects
A major focus for Conservation International is the four-million-acre Beni Biosphere Reserve in Bolivia. CI is working with the Bolivian

government, the Bolivian National Academy of Science, the Bolivian Institute of Ecology, and numerous local groups to set up a management plan for the reserve. The Beni region in Bolivia is home to nomadic Chimane Indians. In December 1988 an affiliate of Chase Manhattan Bank donated $400,000 of the Bolivian debt to CI to be used as a debt-for-nature conversion. Proceeds from this conversion are being used to support environmental education and forest management in the Chimane Forest area of the Beni preserve.

Future Plans

CI signed a long-term assistance agreement with Stanford University in 1988. This agreement involves exchange and training of Costa Rican students and resource managers.

CI's Guatemala program remains in the early stages, but moved ahead significantly in 1989 when an agreement was reached with the Center for Conservation Studies (CECON) at the University of San Carlos. CI will provide financial and technical support to CECON for the study of wildlands in northern Guatemala.

A book will be released by CI in 1991 as the culmination of research data compiled on 3,800 neotropical bird species by a team of four ornithologists.

Membership Information and Volunteer Possibilities

Annual membership in Conservation International is $25, or $30 for families and $15 for students and seniors. Members receive the quarterly newsletter *TROPICUS*, special publications, and opportunities for worldwide travel.

☐ CONSERVATION LAW FOUNDATION OF NEW ENGLAND

3 Joy Street
Boston, MA 02108-1497
(617) 742-2540
Contact: Douglas I. Foy, Esq., Executive Director

History/Goals

The Conservation Law Foundation was established in 1966. This group of fifteen attorneys, scientists, and policy specialists uses the law in the interest of resource management, environmental protection, and public health in the New England area. CLF has a main office in Boston and a branch office in Montpelier, Vermont.

Past Achievements

CLF successfully blocked three attempts by the U.S. government to drill for oil and gas on George's Bank, the world's most productive fishery.

In 1989 CLF and New England Electric System developed a new approach to utility rate setting, making energy-efficiency investments attractive to investors. The proposal has since been accepted by Rhode Island as well.

A three-year-long case against the Massachusetts Military Reservation ended in 1989 with a settlement. The agreement prohibited the military from several polluting practices, such as open munitions burning.

In 1983 CLF initiated a campaign that resulted in the cleanups of several harbors, including Boston Harbor, New Bedford Harbor, and Salem Sound.

Ongoing Projects
The Conservation Law Foundation works with New England utilities to develop programs to reduce energy waste and pollution.

CLF began a campaign in 1989 to protect the 25 million acres of undeveloped property known as the North Woods, spanning northern Maine, New Hampshire, Vermont, and New York.

CLF is evaluating New England's water supply outlook and will identify the costs of supply development and ways to reduce demand, and will propose a model for meeting utility needs.

Future Plans
CLF will continue to look out for the environmental needs and concerns of the New England area, through citizen involvement and litigation. CLF is committed to promoting waste disposal alternatives and to fighting incineration. CLF will continue to advise governmental agencies, testify in proceedings, and provide technical assistance to citizens fighting for environmental standards.

Membership Information and Volunteer Possibilities
Individual annual membership in the Conservation Law Foundation is $30 and includes a quarterly subscription to the *Quarterly Newsletter*. Professional membership is $250 each year and includes CLF's annual case report. There are also $15 student/senior citizen memberships.

Volunteer possibilities within the organization are limited.

☐ THE CONTEXT INSTITUTE
P.O. Box 11470
Bainbridge Island, WA 98110
(206) 842-0216
Contact: Diane Gilman, Associate Director

History/Goals
The Context Institute was founded in 1979 by Diane and Robert Gilman. Founded as the North Olympic Living Lightly Association, it rapidly expanded and broadened its interests. In 1988, NOLLA became The Context Institute with over 4,000 members nationwide.

The Context Institute advocates a humane, sustainable society through "widespread, effective, direct participation." It advocates changes through individual actions, ethical changes, technological changes at home, in the workplace, and in our communities. The institute is a research and education center and serves the general public as well as leaders from across the country.

Past Achievements

The Context Institute has served as consultants on a number of projects. A group of civic leaders and innovators in the Pacific Northwest utilized experts from The Context Institute as design consultants in the development of the Pacific Northwest Social Innovation Support Project. The Institute also served as design consultants in helping Global Action Plan develop a program to empower groups worldwide working to help the environment. During early 1990, The Context Institute served on a panel of futurists gathered by the USDA Extension Service for strategic long-term planning.

The Context Institute also helped found and develop the Foundatin for Soviet American Economic Cooperation, which works to bring together citizen diplomats and business executives from the United States and the USSR who are concerned about the environmental future.

Ongoing Projects

The Context Institute is an ongoing research and educational center. The staff provides a variety of consultation services to individuals and organizations and advises journalists and television producers on developing trends in the sustainability movement.

The Context Institute has also developed The Global Changes Tracking System (GCTS). GCTS identifies trends, innovations, and strategies relevant to global sustainability and disseminates through the institute's publications, computer-mediated seminars, and other services.

The institute publishes *In Context*, a quarterly journal that explores the issues of a sustainable society. Each journal looks at current trends and news, and focuses on an important theme, such as sustainable habitat, gender, cross-cultural experience, transforming education, the ecology of media, and global climate change.

Future Plans

The Context Institute plans to continue working toward a sustainable world through research and education. The institute will continue to publish *In Context* along with other periodic publications and a newsletter. The institute continues to consult on numerous projects and their expertise is requested on an increasing variety of projects.

Membership Information and Volunteer Possibilities

The Context Institute has "sustainers" as well as subscribers. Sustainers, for $35 annually, receive *In Context* along with the *Sustainer* newsletter, and membership in The Context Institute. Subscribers, for $18 per year, receive the quarterly journal. There are special group rates also available.

☐ COOPER ORNITHOLOGICAL SOCIETY

1100 Glendon Avenue, Suite 1400
Los Angeles, CA 90024
(213) 472-7868
Contact: Jim Jennings, Executive Officer

History/Goals
The Cooper Ornithological Society was founded in 1893. The society is named after an ornithologist from California, Dr. J. G. Cooper. The society's main purpose is to advance the knowledge of birds. This objective is met through the observation and study of birds, the encouragement of bird study, conservation of birds and wildlife, and through the publication of ornithological materials. There are currently 2,200 members.

Past Achievements
The society was incorporated in 1934. Since its founding the society has held an annual meeting somewhere in North America, in which research materials are presented and published.

Ongoing Projects
The society publishes a series called *Studies in Avian Biology*. This series, established in 1900, is published at irregular intervals and contains the results of lengthy studies of interest to society members.

Each year monetary awards are made to individuals not holding doctorates who present the best scientific papers at the annual meeting, which is a forum for those interested in birds. Lectures are presented along with films and research information.

Future Plans
The Cooper Ornithological Society will continue to publish materials in the *Studies in Avian Biology* series. The annual meeting continues to be a gathering of those involved in the study of conservation of birds and wildlife.

Membership Information and Volunteer Possibilities
Regular annual membership in the Cooper Ornithological Society is $23. A $25 family membership is available as well as a $15 student membership; life membership is $600. Members receive the quarterly journal, *The Condor*, established by the society in 1899.

Volunteer possibilities inside the organization are limited; however, all members are encouraged to attend the annual meetings.

☐ DEFENDERS OF WILDLIFE

1244 Nineteenth Street, NW
Washington, DC 20036
(202) 659-9510
Contact: M. Rupert Cutler, President

History/Goals

Defenders of Wildlife was founded in 1947 in Washington, D.C. The organization today has over 80,000 members. Defenders was established to protect wild animals and plants, such as the gray wolf, red wolf, Florida panther, grizzly bear, Western yellow-billed cuckoo, desert tortoise, and Kemp's Ridley sea turtle.

Defenders is dedicated to preserving biological diversity, protecting habitats linked by wildlife movement corridors, improving protection of wildlife on public lands, restoring wolves to their natural habitats, reducing marine entanglement and plastic debris, and outlawing poisons and pesticides dangerous to wildlife.

Past Achievements

Defenders sponsored the 1985 "Wolves and Humans" exhibit in Yellowstone Park and at Boise, Idaho. The exhibit was visited by over 250,000 people and won the Natural Resources Council of America Award of Achievement for Education.

In 1988 Defenders was successful in getting Congress to appropriate $10 million for an expansion of the Lower Rio Grande National Wildlife Refuge in Texas, $2 million to purchase land for the new Sacramento River National Wildlife Refuge in California, and $1 million for additions to the Rachel Carson National Wildlife Refuge in Maine.

In 1988 Defenders coordinated the establishment of a network of over 120 wildlife viewing areas on public and private land throughout the state of Oregon. This plan is supposed to help Oregon's tourism industry and provide an economic reason to the state for the continued preservation of habitat areas, as well as provide the public with access to wildlife in their natural habitats.

Defenders helped win a ban to keep livestock from grazing on more than 10,000 acres of BLM-administered tortoise habitat in Nevada in 1988.

Ongoing Projects

Defenders of Wildlife is working with various agencies to reintroduce the red and gray wolves back into their natural habitats. In an effort to encourage acceptance of these animals by livestock producers, Defenders has a compensation program that pays for all verified livestock losses caused by the wolves in the northern Rockies.

Defenders continues to work to alleviate predator poisoning. In several states a livestock guard dog program has been established as an alternative to poisons. Defenders has worked with the Agriculture Department Cooperative Extension Service's pest management program, which encourages nonlethal wildlife control methods. The EPA works with Defenders to operate the "Poison Patrol" hotline, open for anyone suspecting pesticide killing of wildlife.

Defenders also has ongoing programs to prevent entanglement of marine mammals and to reduce the plastic debris found in marine habitats. Defenders is working on a bill to strengthen the national wildlife refuge system.

Future Plans

Defenders will continue in its current focus into the future, and will continue to work through many of its already successful programs. Long-term goals are to protect and restore wildlife habitats, to promote an appreciation for wildlife, and to educate the public on wildlife and natural habitats.

Membership Information and Volunteer Possibilities

Annual membership in Defenders of Wildlife is $20. Reduced memberships are available for students and seniors. Members receive the bimonthly magazine *Defenders*, and receive full voting privileges in choosing the board of directors. Members occasionally receive invitations to special events, and limited-edition wildlife prints.

The Defenders Activist Network consists of over 9,000 individuals who promote Defenders' policies and priorities at the grass roots level. Activists receive action alerts, can attend workshops, and receive the quarterly *Activists Newsletter*. Volunteers are also encouraged to assist in the office of the national headquarters or in any of four regional offices.

☐ DESERT BIGHORN COUNCIL

1500 North Decatur Boulevard
Las Vegas, NV 89108
(602) 621-3845
Contact: Paula Stetka

History/Goals

The Desert Bighorn Council was formed in 1957 and consists of wildlife biologists, scientists, administrators, managers, and others working toward the welfare of bighorn sheep.

The council works to educate the public about the desert bighorn and to help ensure the long-term survival of the sheep through habitat improvement and other means.

Past Achievements

In 1967 the council endorsed a proposal to construct water facilities in the mountain regions of the public domain habitat of the bighorn sheep. In 1972 the council urged that permanent identification of legally taken heads and/or horns of mountain sheep be made by those states where mountain sheep populations exist. This was in an effort to aid law enforcement in those areas.

In 1980 the council supported a resolution calling for the placement of the desert bighorn on New Mexico's endangered species list. In 1981 the council called on the State of Texas to resume the Texas desert bighorn reestablishment program. In 1982 the council supported reclassifying eleven roadless areas within the Anza-Borrego State Park in California as state wilderness areas.

Ongoing Projects

The Desert Bighorn Council works to see that information about the desert bighorn sheep is released to the public through various meetings and other public forums. The council also works to coordinate studies concerning the history, ecology, management, protection, and recreational and economic values of the desert bighorn. The council serves as a clearinghouse of information about the sheep to various organizations, professionals, and individuals. The council also serves as an adviser on questions involving the sheep and its habitat.

The council has an annual meeting in April. Since 1957 the annual meetings have served as a forum for approximately 70 to 100 people. Technical papers are presented by experts in the field, and field trips are taken to the bighorn habitat.

In 1962 the council's technical staff began working on a publication concerning the ecology and management of the desert bighorns. The book, *The Desert Bighorn, Its Life History, Ecology and Management*, was finally published in 1980 and covers such topics as environmental impact statements, the California Desert Plan, legislative proposals, and public lands issues.

Occasionally the Desert Bighorn Council awards an individual or group for outstanding contributions to the study of the desert bighorn. This award is not annual, and is presented when the awards committee believes that an individual deserves the recognition.

Future Plans

The Desert Bighorn Council plans to continue its current programs into the future. It is concentrating on stabilizing and ensuring the survival of desert bighorn populations throughout the animal's historic range. The council is working on improving habitat and relocating the bighorns to meet this objective.

Membership Information and Volunteer Possibilities

Annual membership in the council is $10 and is open to individuals "engaged professionally in management, protection, or scientific study of the desert bighorn." Members receive a copy of the *Desert Bighorn Council Transactions*. Nonmembers can also receive the annual report of transactions by sending $13 to the council.

There are no formal volunteer possibilities within the organization.

☐ DUCKS UNLIMITED

One Waterfowl Way
Long Grove, Illinois 60047
(708) 438-4300
Contacts: Carol J. Mainer, Director of Membership
Programs
John E. Walker, President

History/Goals

Ducks Unlimited was first conceived during the Dust Bowl of the 1930s by a group of sportsmen. The organization was incorporated in 1937 and today has over 500,000 members from all fifty states, Canada, and Mexico. There are currently 4,020 chapters, and some 5,700 events are sponsored annually by Ducks Unlimited.

The main focus of Ducks Unlimited is to develop, preserve, and maintain waterfowl habitat throughout North America and to educate the public on waterfowl management. DU makes its preserves available to members for duck hunting.

Past Achievements

Ducks Unlimited has grown into the world's largest private waterfowl conservation organization. DU was instrumental in implementing the North American Waterfowl Management Plan. This plan, an agreement between Canada and the United States, protects over 5.5 million acres of waterfowl habitat.

Ducks Unlimited has completed over 235 conservation programs and manages over 281,000 acres of land, of which nearly 135,000 acres is wetlands.

Ongoing Projects

The Wetlands America program, established in 1984, has three major components: MARSH (Matching Aid to Restore States Habitat), Habitat USA, and Habitat Inventory and Evaluation. Under these three programs, DU provides funds to fish and game departments throughout the United States for wetlands acquisition; operates a "hands-on" engineering and biological program designed to help restore habitat; and inventories and evaluates wetlands using data from the Landsat 5 satellite.

Ducks Unlimited holds the National Ducks Unlimited Continental Shooting Tournament each year. This event, cosponsored in 1989 by Winchester, GMC Truck, and Budweiser, drew nearly 300 participants. The event is used to raise money to help carry out the wetlands acquisition and protection programs of DU.

Future Plans

Ducks Unlimited will focus more on small and seasonal wetlands and upland nesting cover, as these areas are ideal breeding and nesting areas for waterfowl. Many of these lands are on private property, so DU has begun an enhanced program of cooperation with farmers and ranchers.

DU will open up several full-service regional offices across the United States in addition to the national headquarters and the fund-raising chapters already in existence. Each of these offices will focus on domestic habitat, fund-raising, and communications.

In 1987 DU helped to establish the North American Waterfowl Management Plan. Ducks Unlimited plans to spend $500 million directly on this fifteen-year agreement between the United States and Canada and expects that another $300 million will be necessary to carry out projects deemed necessary under the plan.

Membership Information and Volunteer Possibilities
Annual membership in Ducks Unlimited is $20 and entitles members to receive a year's subscription to the *Ducks Unlimited* magazine.

Over 4,000 volunteer fund-raising chapters of Ducks Unlimited exist across the United States. Members are encouraged to become involved at the local level.

☐ EARTH FIRST!

P.O. Box 5871
Tucson, AZ 85703
(602) 622-1371
Contacts: Judi Barr
John Davis, Journal Editor

History/Goals
In 1980 the Wilderness Society's chief lobbyist, David Foreman, left that group to form Earth First! After ten years, David Foreman announced his plans to leave EF! in August 1990. Although EF! has no formal hierarchy, cofounder Mike Roselle and activist Judi Barr have been considered the group's leaders since Foreman's departure.

A direct-action group, EF! claims to be a movement rather than an organization. The "movement" consists of independent bands of activists across the United States. There are currently chapters in twenty-seven states and in eight other countries, including Poland.

According to its own literature, EF! has a militant style that not everyone may be comfortable with. Tactics have included drilling steel spikes into trees, cutting power lines, putting sugar in the fuel tanks of bulldozers, sitting in trees for prolonged periods, and blocking bulldozers and lumbering equipment. Tactics such as these are carried out in an effort to halt construction and development in wild areas.

Past Achievements
Through civil disobedience and direct action involving theatrical demonstrations, Earth First! has spent the last decade bringing environmental issues to the attention of the world and has a long list of such eye-opening achievements. In 1981, in its first major action after its founding,

EF! "cracked" Glen Canyon Dam by unfurling a 300-foot-long plastic banner over the top of the dam that appeared, at first glance and from a distance, to be a crack.

In 1986 EF! blockaded Fishing Bridge in Yellowstone National Park to protest the destruction of the grizzlies' habitat. Nineteen EF!ers were arrested as a result.

In 1985 EF!ers sat on treetop platforms eighty feet above the ground for nearly a month to protest logging in Willamette National Forest in Oregon.

In October 1986 Texas EF!ers chained themselves to tree crushers to protest logging in Four Notch Wilderness. The Texas group repeated the action in January 1990 to protest construction of Austin's Outer Loop. EF! claims the loop is being constructed illegally, since all federal environmental requirements were never addressed.

A group of EF!ers parachuted into British Columbia in 1988 to disrupt the Canadian government's aerial wolf hunt. In the summer of 1990 Earth First! organized the 1990 Redwood Summer, which involved a series of logging protests throughout the Pacific Northwest.

Ongoing Projects

Earth First! works with groups such as Rainforest Action Network to preserve the rain forests and is working to gain the reintroduction of wolves into their native areas.

The Virginia EF! is currently fighting to preserve the 10,965-acre Laurel Fork Special Management Area of the George Washington National Forest as a part of the National Wilderness Preservation System. Eventually they would like to expand the Wilderness westward and northeastward into West Virginia's Monogahela National Forest and southward and eastward into private land in the Allegheny Mountains, the valley land, and the ridge region, creating a core area of some 30,000 acres.

Future Plans

One of Earth First!'s most far reaching plans for the future calls for the development of a wilderness system encompassing 716 million acres of land, or roughly one-third of the total land area of the forty-eight contiguous United States. Within this wilderness certain guidelines would have to be met, including: no permanent habitation by humans except those people indigenous to the area and living a traditional lifestyle; no mechanized equipment would be allowed; no roads inside the area; no logging, mining, industry, agricultural development, or livestock grazing would be allowed; no use of pesticides or herbicides would be allowed; no fire control; reintroduction of indigenous species and removal of all species not native to the area; dismantling and destruction—or at the very least, abandonment—of all dams, roads, power lines and buildings within the area; no overflights or landing of aircraft; and priority would be given to the preservation of the indigenous species and the ecosystem over all else, including human safety.

Membership Information and Volunteer Possibilities

Earth First! has no official membership. The Earth First! journal, *Earth First! The Radical Environmental Journal*, is available for $20 annually. The paper is published eight times each year on the old pagan European nature holidays: November 1, December 21 or 22, February 2, March 21 or 22, May 1, June 21 or 22, August 1, and September 21 or 22.

Activities within Earth First! are all volunteer. Volunteers participate in EF!'s campaigns and perform everything from tree sitting to protesting to sign carrying to spiking trees. All volunteers work through the local chapters of Earth First!

☐ EARTH ISLAND INSTITUTE

300 Broadway, Suite 28
San Francisco, CA 94133–3312
(415) 788-3666
Contacts: John A. Knox, Executive Director
David Phillips, Executive Director

History/Goals

Earth Island Institute was established in 1982 to develop projects for the "conservation, preservation, and restoration of the global environment." The founder, also the current chairman of the board, was David R. Brower, who also founded Friends of the Earth and the League of Conservation Voters and was the first executive director of the Sierra Club. Earth Island is comprised of over twenty separate projects that work together toward the same goals.

Since its founding, Earth Island has worked to help shape a number of projects, to coordinate fund-raising efforts of the various projects, to provide a public outreach program, and to create a working environment that fosters cooperation between the various projects.

Today there are approximately 32,000 members in Earth Island Institute, and the day-to-day operations are guided by the two executive directors. Earth Island's sibling organization is the Earth Island Action Group, an organization dedicated primarily to legislative advocacy.

Past Achievements

Earth Island Institute created the Rainforest Action Network as one of its projects. That organization has gone on to become one of the largest environmental organizations in the country.

In 1987 Earth Island smuggled a cameraman aboard a tuna boat and recorded the fate of dolphins at the hands of tuna fishermen for the first time.

Earth Island won a lawsuit in the late 1980s requiring that all U.S. Pacific tuna boats have a federal observer on board.

Ongoing Projects

Earth Island Institute is actually a clearinghouse for over twenty individual ongoing projects. Included among them are:

Climate Protection Institute develops educational materials and curricular materials about global climate. The institute publishes the *Greenhouse Gas-ette*.

Conferences on the Fate of the Earth coordinates an ongoing series of international conferences held every other year to examine such issues as the environment, peace, human rights, and economic development.

Environmental Litigation Fund helps individuals and other organizations in exploring the uses of citizen lawsuit provisions in governmental statutes.

Environmental Project on Central America (EPOCA) works within the environmental movement in the United States and with organizations on projects in Central America.

Friends of the Ancient Forest works to educate the public on the old growth forests of the Pacific coast.

Green Alternative Information for Action produces communication materials relating to the United States Green movement. The project publishes the *Green Calendar for Social Change*.

International Marine Mammal Project works to stop the killing of dolphins by the tuna industry, to stop commercial whaling, and to end the use of drift nets throughout the world.

Japan Environmental Exchange sponsors citizen exchanges between environmentalists in the United States and Japan.

Rainforest Health Alliance develops educational materials and programs about the tropical forests; this project focuses primarily on health professionals.

Radio Earth Island produces environmental radio programs that are sent by satellite to radio stations around the world.

Sea Turtle Restoration Project organizes citizens in the United States to work toward the restoration of the endangered sea turtles.

US/USSR Environmental Exchange organizes joint projects between environmentalists in the United States and those in the Soviet Union.

Urban Habitat Program produces educational materials that can be utilized in urban neighborhoods and encourages the creative use of urban space.

Watchfire Productions produces music videos designed to educate the public about environmental issues and to motivate the public to act.

Future Plans

Earth Island Institute will continue to administer the various projects under its guidance, in an effort to bring environmental awareness to the public.

Membership Information and Volunteer Possibilities
Annual membership in Earth Island Institute is $25, and members receive a subscription to the quarterly magazine *Earth Island Journal*, as well as discounts on merchandise and campaign updates.

Earth Island Institute has developed Earth Island Centers throughout the United States and several other countries. These centers serve as organizing points for local grassroots groups and encourage members to circulate Earth Island publications and videos, to become involved in national projects, and to spread the message of Earth Island. There are a large number of volunteer opportunities, specifically within the Environmental Project on Central America and the International Marine Mammal Project. Internships are also available through Earth Island Institute.

☐ EARTHWATCH

680 Mount Auburn Street
P.O. Box 403
Watertown, MA 02272–9104
(617) 926-8200
Contact: Brian A. Rosborough, President

History/Goals
Earthwatch was founded in 1971 to send volunteers around the world to work with scientists helping to save the rain forests and endangered species, studying the effects of pollution, and helping to preserve archeological finds. Earthwatch's mission is to "improve human understanding of the planet, the diversity of its inhabitants, and the processes which affect the quality of life on earth." The scientists around the world that are part of Earthwatch monitor global change, conserve endangered habitats and species, explore the heritages of peoples around the world, and foster international cooperation.

Past Achievements
Since its founding Earthwatch's 23,000 volunteers have supported 1,085 projects in 87 countries. Earthwatch has provided over $15 million in funds and equipment to help solve environmental problems.

Ongoing Projects
Each year Earthwatch sponsors over 100 expeditions around the world. Volunteers pay a share of the project cost and then perform the actual work on the project for approximately two to three weeks.

Projects include: Australia's rain forest canopy; the vanishing rain forests of Mexico; documenting and recording the behavior of Puget Sound's orcas (killer whales); observing and photographing the dolphin groups in Tampa and Sarasota bays, Florida; surveying and documenting an Iron Age settlement in Namibia; excavating and documenting the remains of an 8,000-year-old settlement in Thailand; studying the relationships between the white-tailed deer and the small-mammal populations at the National Zoological Park's Conservation and Research Center in Virginia's Shenandoah Valley. Depending on the project chosen, prices can range from $700 to $2,500. Briefings that give the history of a project, its mission, background of the investigators and staff, goals, logistics, maps, in-country information, and a bibliography of reading materials are available for $25 each.

Future Plans
Earthwatch plans to bring environmental education to schoolchildren. Through various grants and corporate sponsorships, Earthwatch hopes to provide the opportunity for 390 teachers and 250 students between the ages of 16 and 21 to work as apprentices to scientists from 45 countries and 27 states in the United States.

In a unique new program, funded by the Durfee Foundation, Earthwatch plans to give humanists, poets, and writers a chance to work at various research stations to help solve complex problems.

Earthwatch hopes to work with businesses throughout the 1990s to bring employers and employees into environmental decision making.

Membership Information and Volunteer Information
Annual membership in Earthwatch is $25. Members receive a subscription to *Earthwatch Magazine*, published every other month. Members can also order the in-depth expedition briefings and are eligible to join expeditions. Various membership events throughout the year give members the chance to share experiences and meet experts as well as view films and slide shows, and attend lectures all around the country.

☐ THE ELMWOOD INSTITUTE

P.O. Box 5765
Berkeley, CA 94705
(415) 845-4595
Contacts: Fritjof Capra, Founder and President
Philippa Winkler, Executive Director

History/Goals
The Elmwood Institute was founded by Fritjof Capra in 1983 as a think tank to serve as a bridge between ideas and actions. The institute has three major goals: to educate activists and others in the field to see the "larger vision"; to help refine a "new paradigm" in our culture, representing the shift from a mechanistic worldview to a holistic and ecological worldview; and to turn key ideas of the new paradigm into policies at the local and regional levels.

The Elmwood Institute puts forth an idea known as "ecothinking," which encourages an awareness of global interdependence, ecological wisdom, peace and nonviolence, human rights, social and economic justice, personal and social responsibility, grassroots democracy, decentralization of economic and political power, cultural diversity, postpatriarchal consciousness, and ethical and spiritual values. The institute serves as a resource for the Green movement and has an extensive international network of experts and organizations from which it draws its material. The Elmwood Institute has approximately 1,000 members currently.

Past Achievements

Elmwood has sponsored a number of seminars, including a 1989 symposium in Japan that resulted in the founding of a major project, Global File, which is discussed below.

Ongoing Projects

Most of the programs at The Elmwood Institute are ongoing. International public conferences and symposia are the major tools of promoting the new paradigm that the institute envisions. Key ideas are discussed, developed, and eventually presented to the public, in the hopes of implementing them into public policy.

Regional discussion groups, Elmwood Circles, provide a forum for citizens across the country to meet and discuss topics of interest. Elmwood continually promotes gatherings of innovative thinkers and activists, who rarely get the chance to talk together to share ideas.

Global File, developed in 1989, links correspondents in Sweden, Germany, Italy, the United States, New Zealand, and Japan via computer. These correspondents evaluate and compare current ecological practices of businesses and governments all over the world. A charter newsletter, *Global File Monitor,* and reports of the proceedings are available to members.

Future Plans

The Elmwood Institute will continue to act as a think tank and resource base for the world's environmental movement. Elmwood Circles, currently in existence in Los Angeles, Oakland, Marin County, California, and Boston, are envisioned across the country.

Membership Information and Volunteer Possibilities

Annual membership in the Institute is $25, and restricted income memberships are available for $15. Members receive the quarterly *Elmwood Newsletter,* the biannual *Global File Monitor,* and Global File reports. A book list of essential reading as well as audio and video tapes of symposia and conferences are also available to members.

The Elmwood Circles, organized at the local levels, offer opportunities for volunteers. In the circles, members can become involved in environmental issues at the grassroots level. Members are encouraged to form new Elmwood Circles in areas where none currently exist. Members may also volunteer to work in the Elmwood Institute's home office in Berkeley, California.

☐ ELSA WILD ANIMAL APPEAL

P.O. Box 4572
North Hollywood, CA 91617–0572
(818) 761-8387
Contact: A Peter Rasmussen, Jr., General Manager

History/Goals

Elsa Wild Animal Appeal was founded in Kenya, East Africa, and brought to the United States in 1969 by Joy Adamson. Ms. Adamson, author of *Born Free*, and her husband, George, were wildlife conservationists. The Elsa Wild Animal Appeal in the United States is affiliated with branches in Kenya, the United Kingdom, Japan, and Canada. In addition to the office in California, there are two other U.S. regional groups, located in Elmhurst, Illinois, and Lake Charles, Louisiana. There are currently 3,000 youth members and 1,000 adult members.

EWAA is dedicated to wildlife conservation and protection of endangered species and the natural environment. The organization also works toward humane treatment of all animals and helps in the establishment of sanctuaries and wildlife preserves. There are also numerous education projects supported by EWAA.

Past Achievements

The Elsa Wild Animal Appeal worked in California to help institute Proposition 117, the California Wildlife Protection Act. Under this act the hunting of mountain lions in California was banned through the year 2020.

EWAA also worked strongly to prompt the U.S. tuna industry to halt the killing of dolphins. The announcement in 1990 by the three major U.S. tuna canners that no tuna will be purchased, processed, or sold which was obtained at the expense of dolphins was also seen by EWAA as a victory after years of campaigning.

Ongoing Projects

Elsa Wild Animal Appeal works on conservation at all levels. A conservation advisory committee oversees legislation and works with government agencies to ensure wildlife and habitat protection.

EWAA sponsors the Elsa Clubs of America for young people under the age of eighteen. The Elsa Clubs are designed to educate children about their environment and get them actively involved in their environment. EWAA develops wildlife education kits designed primarily for elementary age children, which include fact sheets, research materials, posters, and special projects. Each year the Elsa Clubs answer several hundred letters from schoolchildren requesting information about the environment and endangered species.

EWAA annually sponsors safaris that take members to parts of Africa to witness the wildlife there firsthand. Past trips have included nineteen-day and twenty-one-day safaris to Kenya and Tanzania, with visits to the Serengeti, Mount Kenya, the Samburu Game Reserve, and Amboseli National Park, with views of Mount Kilimanjaro.

Future Plans

Elsa Wild Animal Appeal will continue in its goals to further wildlife and habitat preservation. The educational programs of EWAA will continue to be a major focus of the organization. EWAA will also support its legislative advisory committee and will work to make environmental changes at the legislative level.

Membership Information and Volunteer Possibilities

Adult membership in Elsa Wild Animal Appeal is $15.00 annually. Adult members receive a subscription to the triannual *Born Free News*. Children join the Elsa Clubs of America as "Simba Cubs" for $7.50 annually. Each youth member receives a wildlife kit of their choice, a Born Free badge, and a bumper sticker.

There is no organized volunteer network within EWAA, but teachers can opt to use the wildlife education kits in their classroom, or the kits may be utilized by other volunteer organizations such as Boy Scouts, Girl Scouts, 4-H clubs, and libraries.

☐ ENVIRONMENTAL ACTION

1525 New Hampshire Avenue, NW
Washington, DC 20036
(202) 745-4870
Contact: Ruth Caplan, Executive Director

History/Goals

Environmental Action was founded in 1970 by the founders of the first Earth Day. EA is a political action organization that works to protect the earth's environment through pollution prevention. Environmental Action Foundation is an affiliated program of Environmental Action. EA's current focus is on solid waste, toxic substances, drinking water, recycling, global warming, plutonium production, utility policy, ozone depletion, and acid rain.

Past Achievements

Environmental Action played a major part in the passage of a Superfund law and the federal right-to-know law.

In 1989 EA published *Dynamic Duo: RCRA and SARA Title III*. This handbook was designed to help citizens use the Resource Conservation and Recovery Act and the right-to-know legislation. The book was written primarily for activists and municipal planners and looks at topics such as local emergency procedures and how to reduce toxic threats to communities.

Ongoing Projects

Environmental Action Foundation publishes *Power Line*, an energy news journal for utility activists and policymakers. This journal contains in-depth reports on utilities and major trends affecting consumers and the environment.

EAF's Solid Waste Alternatives Project (SWAP) has become nationally respected for its expertise on solid waste reduction and recycling plans. SWAP reaches a large number of people quarterly through the EAF newsletter, *Wastelines*.

EA's political action committee, EnAct/PAC, supports environmental candidates and routinely releases the Congressional environmental "dirty dozen" list.

EA has an ongoing educational program designed to help citizens learn about the environment and the possible toxic hazards in their surroundings.

One of EA's major projects is the Energy Conservation Coalition. This coalition of twenty national public-interest organizations advocates energy efficiency measures. The coalition promotes state and federal measures to increase energy efficiency, enhance the environment, protect consumers, and increase national security.

Future Plans

Through the Energy Conservation Coalition, Environmental Action is conducting a campaign aimed at improving energy efficiency in the transportation sector.

A focus of Environmental Action and the coalition in the future will be the push for renewable energy sources. ECC will initiate a program aimed at improving renewable technologies and efficiency.

Membership Information and Volunteer Possibilities

Annual membership in Environmental Action is $25. Members receive the bimonthly *Environmental Action Magazine*. Membership in EA is not tax deductible; however, any contributions made to Environmental Action Foundation are tax deductible.

Members are encouraged to work together at the local level to influence Congress and state legislatures on environmental issues.

☐ ENVIRONMENTAL DEFENSE FUND

257 Park Avenue South
New York, NY 10010
(212) 505-2100
Contacts: Frederic D. Krupp, Executive Director
Brenda Kahn, Public Information

History/Goals

The Environmental Defense Fund was established in 1967, and there are approximately 150,000 members currently, making EDF the tenth largest environmental organization in the United States. In 1989 EDF's revenues increased 51 percent from the previous year and membership reached an all-time high. EDF is an organization of lawyers, scientists, and economists working to protect and improve environmental quality and public health. Current emphasis is on nine major points: greenhouse effect; wildlife and habitat; ozone depletion; saving the rain forests; acid rain; water; toxics; Antarctica; and recycling. EDF initiates legal action on environmental matters and conducts public service and education campaigns.

In addition to the national office in New York, there are five regional offices located in Washington, D.C.; Boulder, Colorado; Oakland, California; Richmond, Virginia; and Raleigh, North Carolina.

Past Achievements

Environmental Defense Fund established the Environmental Information Exchange to provide scientific, economic, legal, and regulatory environmental information to various organizations.

Ongoing Projects

EDF has been working with scientists and economists in the Soviet Union and the United States to set up summit meetings to discuss the greenhouse effect. In working toward that same goal, EDF works with the United Nations World Climate Conference.

EDF works to save sea turtles and porpoises and pushes for more protection of all endangered species.

EDF works with scientists, economists, and lawyers to create unique, workable solutions to the world's environmental problems. The main focus of EDF's actions is on research, public education, and administrative and legislative action.

Future Plans

The Environmental Defense Fund plans to work toward an international agreement aimed at radically reducing greenhouse gases and implementation of the new standards.

EDF plans to work during the 1990s to save the rain forests, through additional reserves in Brazil as well as new reserves in Indonesia and India. EDF targets development banks in its campaigns, attempting to force the banks to invest in rain forest conservation instead of destruction.

EDF wants to establish nationwide curbside recycling programs and expand the markets for recycled goods. EDF hopes that by the year 2000 at least 50 percent of all trash in the United States will be recycled. EDF also plans to call for new clean water standards and national toxics disclosure laws.

Environmental Defense Fund will attend meetings around the world to voice concerns over Antarctica. EDF wants an Antarctica treaty with strong environmental safeguards for the continent, and seeks to have the continent designated as a world park.

Membership Information and Volunteer Possibilities

Annual membership in Environmental Defense Fund is $20. Members receive the *EDF Letter*, a bimonthly newsletter that reports on EDF's activities.

Members are encouraged to become involved at the local level by working within the community, boycotting endangered animal products, buying products produced in the rain forests, conserving electricity, using phosphate-free detergents and avoiding pesticides, recycling and reusing products, and by writing to U.S. and U.N. officials to encourage them to support environmental initiatives. Limited summer internships are available to students.

☐ FRIENDS OF ANIMALS

P.O. Box 1244
Norwalk, CT 06856
(203) 866-5223
Contacts: Priscilla Feral, President
Robert Roehr, Public Relations
Regina B. Frankenberg, National Adviser

History/Goals

Friends of Animals was established in 1957 and today has over 120,000 members nationwide. FoA works to "reduce and eliminate the suffering inflicted by humans upon nonhuman animals." Along with the national headquarters in Connecticut, FoA has a corporate office in New York City, and branch offices in Miami, Florida; Newport, Rhode Island; Washington, D.C.; San Diego, California; and Paris, France.

Past Achievements

In 1989 FoA launched a successful anti-fur campaign entitled "Get a Feel for Fur, Slam Your Fingers in a Car Door." This slogan was seen throughout the year on billboards, sides of buses, and phone kiosks in New York City.

FoA has established a wild animal orphanage and rehabilitation center in Liberia.

FoA has also established the Committee for Humane Legislation in Washington, D.C. This separately incorporated organization is the lobbying arm of Friends. The committee works to change unsatisfactory laws, to ensure enactment and enforcement of current protective laws, and to help drive new legislation through Congress.

Ongoing Projects

Friends of Animals has several ongoing programs, focusing on such issues as breeding control, wildlife and marine mammal protection,

protection of animals used in lab experiments, and the protection of farm animals.

FoA is currently working to reverse the 1982 decision made by the U.S. Fish and Wildlife Service that legalized swan hunting in the United States.

FoA is working with animal protectionists to publicize the treatment of greyhounds used for racing. FoA is a member of the No Dog Track Coalition in Bridgeport, Connecticut, which has been fighting to keep a greyhound track out of that city.

FoA works to protect dolphins and protests the conditions at dolphin petting pools around the country. FoA has worked with groups such as Dolphin Project to protest the keeping of dolphins in captivity.

Future Plans

Friends is working to produce a video about American fur farms. FoA plans to show the video to millions of American viewers as part of its antifur campaign. The antifur campaign will remain one of FoA's largest projects.

Friends of Animals convinced the U.S. Army, which was going to have to abandon a large number of trucks as troops pulled out of Europe, to donate several trucks to FoA. The thirty-four large Dodge M-880 trucks will be refurbished as antipoaching patrol vehicles, to be used to help combat ivory poaching in East Africa. FoA envisions an eventual fleet of over 100 patrol trucks, with over 1,000 park rangers patrolling the fields in East Africa.

Friends will continue with its programs into the future. The organization plans to focus on educating the public about the fur industry and will work to protect captive dolphins.

Membership Information and Volunteer Possibilities

Annual membership in Friends of Animals is $20. Reduced memberships are available for students, seniors, and handicapped persons at $10 annually. Members receive a year's subscription to the quarterly magazine, *Act'ion Line*, along with Action Alerts.

Volunteers are heavily relied on by Friends. There are volunteer advisers in forty-one states across the United States. These volunteers clip newspapers for articles, participate in local activities, and initiate other activities on behalf of FoA. Volunteers are encouraged to write letters and respond to other calls to action through the Action Alerts. Volunteers also work with the breeding control program and in other projects at the local level.

☐ FRIENDS OF THE EARTH

218 D Street, SE
Washington, DC 20003
(202) 544-2600
Contacts: Michael S. Clark, Executive Director
Beth Stein, Public Information Coordinator

History/Goals

Friends of the Earth was founded in 1969 by David Brower, who also founded Earth Island Institute and the League of Conservation Voters and served as the Sierra Club's first executive director. In 1990 Friends of the Earth merged with the Oceanic Society, which had been founded in 1969, and Environmental Policy Institute, which was founded in 1972. There are currently 50,000 members in Friends of the Earth, with offices in Washington, D.C., Seattle, and Manila, Philippines, as well as thirty-eight international affiliates. The current president is Michael Clark, formerly of the Environmental Policy Institute.

According to FOE's mission statement, Friends of the Earth is a "global advocacy organization that works at local, national, and international levels to: protect the planet, preserve biological, cultural, and ethnic diversity; and empower citizens to have a voice in decisions affecting their environment and lives."

FOE currently focuses on seven major topics: ozone depletion, tropical forest destruction, oceans and coasts, global warming, solid and hazardous waste, nuclear weapons production, and corporate accountability. The organization continues to use the Oceanic Society to identify its lobbying and publication efforts. Although each group located throughout the world is independent, an international secretariat in London links the organizations through an international newsletter (FOELink) as well as through regular meetings of an executive committee and an annual international conference.

Past Achievements

Since its founding and in conjunction with other groups, Friends of the Earth has helped protect 103 million acres of land in the Arctic National Wildlife Refuge.

FOE has successfully opposed the construction of nuclear power plants and stopped a billion-dollar federal subsidy to the Synthetic Fuels Corporation.

FOE has investigated the radioactive wastes generated by America's sixteen nuclear weapons production facilities, and has helped spread word of the contamination to the American public.

Ongoing Projects

Friends of the Earth is participating with Paul McCartney, Capitol Records, and Pollack Media Group in "Rescue the Future." This campaign is designed to urge the public to support a ban on the production and use of all ozone-destroying chemicals.

FOE-UK and FOE-Malaysia are working together on a campaign aimed at reforming the tropical timber trade and protecting the native forest dwellers.

FOE-Italy has organized a campaign that assists environmental groups in the Soviet Union and Eastern Europe with organizing efforts, printing and supplies, and technical information.

FOE conducts international campaigns focusing on global warming and ozone depletion. The organization is also working to involve more minorities in environmental policymaking.

Friends of the Earth also distributes informational fact sheets and brochures to increase public awareness of environmental problems.

Future Plans

Friends of the Earth will continue working through its international offices to focus on global environmental problems. FOE has set numerous priorities for the future: to restore the rain forests, heal the eroding ozone layer, keep the oceans clean, demand corporate accountability, reduce hazardous and solid waste, and eliminate nuclear weapon production.

Membership Information and Volunteer Possibilities

Annual membership in Friends of the Earth is $25. Members receive a subscription to the newsmagazine *Not Man Apart*, discounts on merchandise and publications, as well as a membership kit highlighting FOE's activities and information on how to become more involved. FOE also publishes *Atmosphere*, an ozone newsletter; *Community Plume*, a chemical safety newsletter; and *Groundwater News*, a newsletter.

Members can volunteer to be activist members and become involved at the local level in environmental issues. There are fact sheets to help members adopt environmentally sound habits in their daily lives. Internships are available to college students.

☐ FRIENDS OF THE SEA OTTER

P.O. Box 221220
Carmel, CA 93922
(408) 625-3290
Contacts: Carol Fulton, Executive Director
Julia Wenner, Membership Secretary

History/Goals

Friends of the Sea Otter is a trust that was formed in 1968 by a group of conservationists, scientists, lawyers, photographers, and divers. The major goal of the group is the protection of the sea otter population along the California coast. There are over 4,700 members from fifty states and fourteen countries.

Past Achievements

Experts from the Friends of the Sea Otter were called upon to testify for the Endangered Species and Marine Mammal Protection acts in Washington, D.C., and the group has succeeded in having the southern sea otter listed as a threatened species. The friends have helped to secure the reintroduction of the sea otter to its ancestral home on San Nicolas Island in Southern California. The friends have helped the Fish and Wildlife Service count otters during censuses and have rescued stranded otters.

Ongoing Activities

The Friends of the Sea Otter operate an educational center in Carmel, California. The center is open to the public daily and is also a source of scientific material for students, authors, and the public. The friends meet with administrators from both the Department of Fish and Game and the U.S. Fish and Wildlife Service to observe the work of their biologists and to follow their progress.

Future Plans

Friends of the Sea Otter is working to reduce threats to the otters from gill netting, coastal pollution, oil spills, and random killings. The group will continue in its goal of being a voice for the sea otters.

Membership Information and Volunteer Possibilities

General membership in Friends of the Sea Otter is $20 annually. There is a reduced membership for students and seniors at $15 per year and a lifetime membership of $125. Members receive updates on sea otters and a subscription to the *Raft*, the group's newsletter.

Volunteers help run the educational center and often make educational presentations in the area concerning the sea otters.

☐ GLOBAL TOMORROW COALITION

1325 G Street, NW, Suite 915
Washington, DC 20005–3104
(202) 628-4016
Contacts: Donald R. Lesh, President
Diane G. Lowrie, Vice President

History/Goals

The Global Tomorrow Coalition was established in 1981 and unites over 120 nongovernmental organizations, educational institutions, corporations, and concerned individuals. The coalition was formed to tackle problems such as population growth, resource consumption, environmental degradation, and unsustainable development. GTC serves as a clearinghouse for various groups and publishes materials that can be used in forming public policy or by those working at the grassroots level.

GTC's goal is to "contribute to broader public understanding of the interaction of long-term global trends in population, resources, environment, and development, and to help promote informed and responsible public choice among alternative futures for the United States and alternative roles for the nation within the international community."

Past Achievements

GTC published *The Global Ecology Handbook: What You Can Do About the Environmental Crisis.* This handbook provides facts about global population, resource depletion, and environmental problems; it shows how these problems are connected and how they affect the lives of people throughout the world. The handbook goes on to demonstrate how the problems are being dealt with, then proposes solutions and gives further sources of information and assistance.

The coalition has also developed a global issues education set. This set, for both elementary and secondary levels, has six units: Sustainable Development, Biological Diversity, A Global Awakening, Marine and Coastal Resources, Population, and Tropical Forests. Lesson plans and activities are included. The set encourages classroom participation, hands-on activities, group discussions, role-playing, simulations, and creativity. A copy of *The Global Ecology Handbook* is included in the set.

GTC has served as a resource consultant to Rotary International in the development of their program in 1990 entitled Preserve Planet Earth (PPE).

For Earth Day 1990 GTC funded several Earth Day programs in elementary schools in California.

The coalition helped establish and will help manage the International Network for Environmental Policy (INEP). INEP is a computer network and data base designed for use by national parliaments, nongovernmental organizations, corporations and other businesses, national governments, those in science and academia, local and state-level governments, and international bodies.

Ongoing Projects

The 1990 Public Broadcasting Service series, "Race to Save the Planet," by WGBH Television in Boston, is the basis for several ongoing projects of the coalition. For community groups, GTC has developed the *Community Discussion Guide* to accompany the series. The series has been made available on videotape for rental by community groups and others wishing to study it. The *Community Discussion Guide* will provide synopses of the ten programs, a review of terms and concepts, questions for discussion and brainstorming, and other information that could be utilized in a discussion format. The guide is designed to supplement the

GTC Global Ecology Handbook and its predecessor, *Citizen's Guide to Sustainable Development.*

Also in conjunction with the PBS series, GTC has published the *Race to Save the Planet Environmental Education Activity Guide.* This thirty-two-page guide is designed for use throughout the high school curriculum and offers classroom activities, discussion questions, and readings and further resources. There is also a pull-out reproducible section aimed at getting students involved in environmental issues at the local level.

Global Tomorrow Coalition works to establish Global Issues Resource Centers nationwide. These centers are designed to provide a library of circulating materials such as periodicals, speeches, current policy analyses, cassette tapes, videos, curriculum materials, and slide shows.

GTC works with the United Nations, several Third World nongovernmental organizations, and the U.S. Congress to bring about changes in current environmental policy.

Future Plans

GTC is compiling college course outlines on global issues. These outlines will make the basis for a GTC college guide to accompany the *Global Ecology Handbook* at the university level.

The coalition has recently completed a feasibility study on an alert network on global issues. The program, GIANT, is planned for implementation in the future. GTC will strive to make information available to the public and policy makers concerning sustainable development in the United States and throughout the world.

Membership Information and Volunteer Possibilities

Membership in the Global Tomorrow Coalition is broken down into two categories: participating member and affiliate member. A participating member is an organization. Those organizations that choose to become participating members attend an annual meeting, elect GTC officers and the board of directors, and provide counsel on goals and policies of GTC. Affiliate members are those organizations and individuals who share the concerns of GTC but do not vote in the annual meeting. Individual affiliate memberships are available for $35 annually, or $15 for students and seniors.

There are no formal volunteer programs other than any community groups that are formed utilizing the GTC information. Internships are available in legislation research and global issues forums.

☐ GRAND CANYON TRUST
The Homestead
Route 4, Box 718
Flagstaff, AZ 86001
(602) 774-7488
Contact: Office Manager

History/Goals

The Grand Canyon Trust was established in 1985 in the State of Arizona. There is also an office in Washington, D.C. Currently there are 2,000 members. The trust was established to help preserve, conserve, and manage the public lands, water, wildlife, and other natural resources for the Colorado Plateau located in portions of Wyoming, Colorado, Utah, Arizona, and New Mexico.

The trust's major roles are to provide a long-range plan for the Colorado Plateau; to help governments at all levels develop and implement sound management policies; to monitor the government agencies administering the lands in the Colorado Plateau; and to seek change in Congress and in the state legislatures, or in the courts if necessary.

To fulfill its goals the trust identifies and spreads information concerning the preservation of the Colorado Plateau, provides information to analysts and decision makers at all levels as well as the media, works with all parties concerned (landowners, land users, and community and state representatives) to set up long-range plans for the areas within the Colorado Plateau, and oversees all decisions affecting the area.

Past Achievements

The Grand Canyon Trust has been conducting research and providing information to legislatures and other policy makers since its founding. In 1989 the Secretary of the Interior, Manuel Lujan, called for an environmental impact statement on Glen Canyon Dam operations. Following his order, a series of public hearings was held in the spring of 1990. Grand Canyon Trust was actively involved in these proceedings, and it had been getting information out to the public prior to the actual hearings.

Ongoing Projects

The Grand Canyon Trust became a member of the Utah Wilderness Coalition in 1990 in an effort to help support the Utah Bureau of Land Management (BLM) Wilderness bill. That bill would set aside 5.1 million acres of Utah land as wilderness. GTC will continue to help disseminate information on this issue and others like it.

Each year the Grand Canyon Trust coordinates river trips on the Colorado River in the Grand Canyon. The trips, with commercial river outfitters, are open to members and give them a chance to see what is actually at stake in the Grand Canyon.

Future Plans

The Grand Canyon Trust is working on several major projects that will go on for some time. The trust is concerned with the pollution levels in the Grand Canyon as well as the effect the Glen Canyon Dam operations will have on the Colorado Plateau if "peaking power" electricity is generated from the dam.

The trust is also working on the resource management plan for a 2.8-

million-acre strip of land in Arizona known as the Arizona Strip. The BLM is finalizing a resource management plan in the area.

Membership Information and Volunteer Possibilities

Annual membership in the Grand Canyon Trust is $25. Members of the trust receive the *Colorado Plateau Advocate*, the trust's quarterly journal. Those making larger donations receive additional gifts, such as photographs and books. There are no volunteer positions available within the organization.

☐ GREATER YELLOWSTONE COALITION

P.O. Box 1874
Bozeman, MT 59771
(406) 586-1593
Contacts: Edward Lewis, Executive Director
Ken Barrett, Membership and Development
Director

History/Goals

The Greater Yellowstone Coalition is a group of twelve national organizations and over sixty regional member organizations that was formed in 1983 to protect and preserve the Greater Yellowstone ecosystem. This ecosystem is comprised of approximately 14 million acres covering Yellowstone and Grand Teton national parks, seven national forests, three national wildlife refuges, BLM holdings, and over one million acres of privately owned land. The coalition seeks to concentrate on the natural boundaries of the region rather than the manmade boundaries. The coalition meets those goals through grassroots activism, scientific study, and public education.

Past Achievements

The coalition has seen significant results since its founding. In 1988 the coalition won congressional approval of legislation designed to protect the Corwin Springs Known Geothermal Area. The coalition persuaded Phillips Petroleum not to drill for oil on the Line Creek Plateau in the Beartooth Mountains. The coalition's actions forced an end to the Forest Service's timber sales in the Targhee and Gallatin national forests to preserve the grizzlys' habitat.

Lobbying by the coalition and other national environmental organizations brought positive changes to the 1988 Oil and Gas Leasing Reform Bill, calling for greater public input into the leasing decisions.

The coalition worked with The Wilderness Society to get improvements in the platinum exploration proposal for the East Boulder River. The improvements require that habitat considered essential for spawning cutthroat trout, wintering bald eagles, and mule deer be monitored closely.

The coalition put together a Yellowstone Grizzly Bear Status Report as a result of a special study that consolidated the previously existing habitat and mortality data on the grizzly populations in Yellowstone. The status report is a major tool in managing current bear populations and planning for the future.

Ongoing Projects
The coalition hosts a scientific conference and annual meeting in Yellowstone National Park. This conference is designed to educate the public and current members about issues concerning the Yellowstone ecosystem.

The coalition works to stop the oil drilling that is currently allowed or the drilling that is under application in nearly five million acres of the Yellowstone ecosystem.

The coalition is also working to stop mining, which it considers responsible for acid runoff, heavy metals contamination, sedimentation, and erosion in the ecosystem.

Future Plans
The Greater Yellowstone Coalition will continue in its efforts to protect the entire Yellowstone ecosystem, or greater Yellowstone. A five-year initiative has been launched, called Greater Yellowstone Tomorrow. This initiative will eventually provide a working blueprint for the entire ecosystem to protect the wildlife, fisheries, scenic landscapes, and geothermal sites.

Membership Information and Volunteer Possibilities
Annual membership in the Greater Yellowstone Coalition is $25. Members receive a subscription to the quarterly newsletter, *Greater Yellowstone Report*, and action alerts to keep up-to-date on issues.

Volunteer opportunities are available through the coalition as well as the member organizations. Members are encouraged to write letters and to assist the coalition staff in special community events and projects.

☐ GREENPEACE U.S.A.
1436 U Street, NW
Washington, DC 20009
(202) 462-1177
Contact: Peter Bahouth, Executive Director

History/Goals
Greenpeace was started in 1971 in British Columbia, Canada, by a small group of people opposed to nuclear testing on Amchitka Island in Alaska. Today Greenpeace is an international organization dedicated to preserving the earth and its life. Greenpeace continues to work to stop the threat of nuclear war and the production of nuclear weapons, but it now goes much further. Greenpeace also works to protect the environ-

ment from toxic pollutants, to stop the threat of greenhouse warming, and to arrest the depletion of the ozone layer. The group has actively worked to halt the killing of whales, dolphins, seals, and other endangered land and sea animals.

Greenpeace believes in taking direct, nonviolent action to bring about change. The organization also has investigators who study the scientific, financial, and political sides of problems. Greenpeace today has offices in Argentina, Australia, Austria, Belgium, Canada, Costa Rica, Denmark, Germany, France, Ireland, Italy, Japan, Luxembourg, the Netherlands, New Zealand, the Soviet Union, Spain, Sweden, Switzerland, the United Kingdom, and the United States. The doubling of membership during 1988 and 1989 to the current level of 2.3 million members has made Greenpeace the largest of all the environmental organizations. The group receives $40 million annually from its members and has an annual budget of over $50 million.

Past Achievements

In 1989 Greenpeace led a boycott against Iceland to protest that country's continued whaling practices. The boycott was successful, and Iceland halted the killing of whales.

The first nongovernmental scientific camp was established in the Antarctic in 1987 by Greenpeace.

When Greenpeace discovered that the Ciba-Geigy Corporation's plant in Toms River, New Jersey, had been discharging industrial chemicals into the ocean and illegally dumping wastes on its property for years, the organization initiated direct actions against the corporation and an education campaign to alert the public. The result was over thirty criminal indictments of plant officials, fines of $4.5 million, and orders to shut down the ocean pipeline from the Toms River plant by January 1992.

Ongoing Projects

The Greenpeace Toxics Campaign works to bring the issue of toxic wastes to the public's attention. Greenpeace encourages citizens to demand the implementation and government enforcement of toxic waste prevention policies by industries.

Greenpeace opposes nuclear weapons at sea and has a long-established policy of blocking nuclear-armed ships from entering neutral ports. The organization also carries out research into the effects of nuclear accidents on sea life and distributes the findings to the public.

In 1987 Greenpeace established a sister organization called Greenpeace Action. Greenpeace Action carries out direct actions, research, and public education programs, and mobilizes grassroots volunteers to pressure legislators at the local, state, and federal levels.

Future Plans

Greenpeace has many definite goals for the future. The group hopes to maintain the International Whaling Commission moratorium on commercial whaling through the year 2000 and to stop "research whaling" by Japan. The organization wants Antarctica declared a world park to preserve the vast continent and its animals and resources. Greenpeace will push to establish recycling programs nationwide, to encourage the use of recycled materials, and to discontinue styrofoam and other plastics.

In 1989 the Atmosphere and Energy Campaign was launched. This long-term campaign will push for changes to protect the global atmosphere. Within the campaign, Greenpeace hopes to stop the production and use of chlorofluorocarbons (CFCs); to dramatically reduce the level of pollution in the United States; to increase fuel economy of U.S. automobiles and to encourage improvements in transportation systems; to encourage energy efficiency in all aspects of life; to encourage a switch to renewable energy resources; and to encourage trade patterns that take development and progress of renewable energy sources into consideration.

Membersip Information and Volunteer Opportunities
Membership in Greenpeace is $15 annually. Members receive the bimonthly magazine, *Greenpeace.* Members of Greenpeace are encouraged to take an active volunteer role in the organization.

Greenpeace has five U.S. regional offices, in Illinois, Massachusetts, Florida, California, and Washington, D.C. These regional offices, all part of the global Greenpeace effort in twenty-three countries, provide a base for this country's members. Greenpeace has a fleet of seven ships, fifty inflatable boats, and two campaign buses to transport active members to places where direct action campaigns are planned. Members can participate by joining boycotts, making nonviolent protests, campaigning for Greenpeace-backed programs, or helping in any other number of activities that the organization plans throughout the year. Activities at the local level are often organized through Greenpeace Action.

☐ HAWK MOUNTAIN SANCTUARY ASSOCIATION
Route 2
Kempton, PA 19529
(215) 756-6961
Contacts: Stanley E. Senner, Executive Director
June A. Trexler-Kuhns, Membership Secretary
James J. Brett, Curator

History/Goals
Hawk Mountain Sanctuary was established in 1934 to help in the conservation of birds of prey and other wildlife. The sanctuary was originally established to stop the shooting of hawks, eagles, ospreys, and falcons as

they migrated over Hawk Mountain annually. Each year over 24,000 raptors of 14 different species now pass over Hawk Mountain.

The sanctuary is located in eastern Pennsylvania on a 2,200-acre refuge. There are currently over 8,000 members.

Past Achievements

The sanctuary has become a visitor attraction. In 1988 over 46,000 visitors arrived at the sanctuary from forty-eight states, the District of Columbia, and twenty-five foreign countries.

Hawk Mountain was a key player in the efforts to gain legal protection for birds of prey in the United States and continues to be an advocate for conservation policies.

Hawk Mountain has carried out various kinds of research through a variety of projects. During 1989, one project involved the "marking" of red-tails to enable researchers to observe how many birds stayed on Hawk Mountain and how many left the area. Another 1989 project involved attaching radio transmitters to five red-tails. Researchers then followed the five hawks south, focusing on their behavior as they migrated.

During early 1990 Hawk Mountain published a summary of the entire fifty-three-year history of research projects undertaken at the sanctuary. This publication contains much information about raptor populations and monitoring techniques.

Ongoing Projects

The major ongoing project of the sanctuary is maintaining the refuge itself. The refuge is open year-round. The visitor's center has exhibits and a gift shop. During the fall there are lectures along the trail. Guided programs for organizations and school groups are available year-round. The Habitat Trail, which includes two ponds, waterfalls, a marsh, and wildflowers and shrubs is wheelchair-accessible via a brick walkway. There are numerous workshops, trips, and special events throughout the year. On Saturday nights during the fall, there is an "under the stars" lecture series featuring naturalists and photographers. Special courses are also offered for college credit throughout the year in conjunction with Cedar Crest College in Allentown, Pennsylvania.

There are ongoing monitoring projects at the sanctuary, many involving interns and visiting scientists.

Future Plans

The sanctuary plans to continue its operation of the refuge and visitor's center. The sanctuary will continue to focus on environmental education as well as research, and will continue to support conservation policies.

Membership Information and Volunteer Possibilities

Annual Membership in the Hawk Mountain Sanctuary is $20. Members receive *The Hawk Mountain News*, an annual report, and other special publications. Members also have free admission to the trail and the lookouts (normal admission is $3.00 for adults and $1.50 for children), plus discounts on educational special events.

There is a large volunteer network at the sanctuary. Currently over 200 people are active volunteers. Volunteers help with hawk counts, mailings, and maintenance. In 1982 the volunteer program was expanded beyond these functions, and today volunteers can also assist in making school presentations, operating the bookstore, weeding and planting in the gardens, maintaining the library, helping the researchers, caring for the educational birds, solving computer problems, fund-raising, designing brochures, helping at special functions, and helping in the office or in other capacities to support the staff. Volunteers recorded a total of 3,247 hours in 1989.

☐ THE HUMANE SOCIETY OF THE UNITED STATES

2100 L Street, NW
Washington, DC 20037
(202) 452-1100
Contact: John A. Hoyt, President

History/Goals
The Humane Society of the United States was founded in 1954 to prevent the abuse of animals. With over one million members today, HSUS provides information and does investigative legislative and educational work to ensure the safety of all animals—on the farm, in research labs, at pet shops and breeders, on racetracks, and those in the wild.

Past Achievements
In 1989 HSUS helped organize the Global Cetacean Coalition. HSUS then hosted the ad hoc group of forty national and international organizations that strive to extend the global moratorium on commercial whaling to the year 2000 and to stop the killing of cetaceans in nets.

A booklet, *A Practical Guide to Humane Control of Wildlife in Cities and Towns,* was published by HSUS to help animal control agents and laypeople solve wildlife-related problems.

A lawsuit filed by the Humane Society was effective in stopping a program in California's Mojave Desert that would have poisoned thousands of ravens.

Ongoing Projects
The Humane Society's "Shame of Fur" campaign has been successful since it inception in 1988 in pressuring the fur industry and educating fur consumers on the cruelty of fur fashions. The campaign is active nationwide.

The HSUS farm animals and bioethics staff monitored the reliance on drugs to make animals more productive on large livestock and poultry farms. HSUS is working with farmers to introduce organic farming and safer farming practices.

The Humane Society companion animals division provides support for shelters across the United States. Specialized workshops and seminars are offered to assist those in the shelters and the community in learning how to care for animals.

The ongoing "Be a P.A.L.—Prevent a Litter" campaign promotes the importance of spaying and neutering. This effort has been successfully undertaken since 1987.

HSUS also has an active field services division and investigations department, both of which track and investigate handling of animals by slaughterhouses, pet shops, zoos, circuses, and shelters across the country.

The Humane Society general counsel's office provides legal assistance, support, and litigation services to other HSUS departments and programs.

Future Plans

The Humane Society of the United States plans to pursue these same goals in the future, and to prevent the abuse of all animals. HSUS hopes to shut down the fur fashion industry, stop the killing of whales, and reduce the number of unwanted animals born each year, and will continue its attempts to rescue animals in trouble.

Membership Information and Volunteer Possibilities

Individual membership in the Humane Society of the United States is $10, and $18 for families. Members vote on the twenty-four-member board of directors and receive the quarterly *HSUS News* along with periodic Close-Up Reports on major issues. *Shelter Sense* is a newsletter for professionals in shelters and animal control.

The Humane Society encourages members at the local level to become involved in the campaigns and to help bring the goals of the HSUS to communities across the country.

☐ INFORM

381 Park Avenue South
New York, NY 10016
(212) 689-4040
Contacts: Joanna D. Underwood, President
Wendy Leavens, Communications Assistant

History/Goals

INFORM was established in 1973 by environmental research specialist Joanna Underwood and two of her colleagues. The three had a strong concern about air pollution and envisioned an organization that would identify practical ways to protect the environment and public health.

INFORM's research is recognized nationwide and used by legislators, conservation groups, and business leaders in shaping environmental policies and programs.

INFORM's research currently focuses on four major topics: hazardous waste reduction, solid waste management, urban air pollution, and land and water conservation. INFORM does no lobbying or litigating but rather provides information resulting from research in the form of books, abstracts, newsletters, and articles.

Past Achievements

INFORM's first project was *A Clear View*, published in 1975. This research publication was a guide for local groups, showing them how to investigate industrial pollution and what could be done about it. This book has since been used as a textbook in more than twelve colleges nationwide, is a reference book for the Environmental Defense Fund and numerous other smaller organizations, and was utilized by Shell Oil and International Paper in establishing new air pollution policies.

In 1982 INFORM began what was to become a three-year study on toxic waste practices in the chemical industry in the United States. The 530-page report, *Cutting Chemical Wastes*, was used by Congress during the shaping of the nation's first federal legislation on waste reduction. The report also initiated the creation of the EPA's Office of Pollution Prevention.

INFORM has published numerous consumer manuals aiding prospective retirement lot purchasers in the Sunbelt states in distinguishing between legitimate deals and false claims.

INFORM has also conducted studies concerning the new technologies available to allow the cleaner burning of coal. Studies in workplace health and safety have focused on the U.S. copper industry, and a directory has been published listing clinics across the country specializing in the treatment of job-related illnesses and injuries.

Ongoing Projects

INFORM has an active staff of 22 full-time scientists and researchers along with approximately twelve volunteers and college interns. Research projects are ongoing. Publications reporting the results of research to the public are released as they are completed.

INFORM has been working with farmers throughout the Southwest to introduce a new irrigation management method. The suggestions and research results of INFORM are currently being expanded by the U.S. Soil Conservation Service through a grant from the California Energy Commission.

INFORM has an active outreach program aimed at educating the public. INFORM staff members make presentations at national and international conferences and at workshops. Staffers have given briefings and testimony at congressional hearings and have made television and radio appearances to increase public awareness.

Future Plans

INFORM is planning to publish a step-by-step manual targeted toward grassroots organizations. This book, to be titled *A Citizen's Guide to Promoting Toxic Waste Reduction*, will be a research source for local groups.

INFORM will also be publishing a directory of organizations concerned with hazardous chemicals and will offer a summary of the groups' views and suggested policies.

INFORM will concentrate some efforts in the future on natural gas and methanol programs. A research project detailing practical and technical information on existing programs and follow-up reports on future needs is planned. These reports can then be utilized by policy makers, corporate executives, and citizens' groups in the United States.

Membership Information and Volunteer Possibilities

Annual membership in INFORM is $25. Members receive a one-year subscription to *INFORM Reports*, the quarterly newsletter. For an annual donation of $50, members will also receive a string shopping bag and will be an INFORMed shopper. For contributions of $100 or more, members also receive a discount on new INFORM studies. There are currently over forty major studies available to members, and new studies are published on an ongoing basis.

Volunteer positions are available to assist staff researchers and aid in the administrative areas of the organization. There are also internships available to college students.

☐ THE INSTITUTE FOR EARTH EDUCATION

P.O. Box 288
Warrenville, IL 60555
(708) 393-3096 or (509) 395-2299
Contacts: Bruce Johnson, International Program
Coordinator
Dave Wampler, Institute Coordinator

History/Goals

The Institute for Earth Education was established in 1974 to provide a serious educational response to the environmental crisis. The institute serves educators around the world through its offices in the United States, Canada, Britain, France, Australia, and New Zealand. The institute works closely with educators to design environmental learning programs. There are currently 2,000 members, including concerned individuals as well as educators.

Past Achievements

IEE has developed complete educational programs for students. The Sunship Earth, Earthkeepers, and Earth Caretakers programs developed for children from ten to fourteen years of age are in place and being utilized in five countries.

IEE has also developed an extensive list of educational supplements and workshops for teachers in all grade levels.

Ongoing Projects

The Institute regularly conducts workshops and teacher training programs, hosts international conferences, and publishes material on an ongoing basis.

IEE is working on the first stages of implementing a new project, Lost Treasures, designed for eight- and nine-year-olds, and is working on the publication of Sunship III, a new program for thirteen- and fourteen-year-old students.

Throughout the world, the Institute for Earth Education has developed international sharing centers where educators and others interested in earth education can go to see the programs and activities firsthand. The centers are chosen because of their excellent earth education programs. Each site has an associate staff member on hand to assist the programs and to answer visitors' questions. In the United States, some of the sites are: Battle Creek Outdoor Education Center in Dowling, Michigan; Heller Nature Center in Highland Park, Illinois; Manzano Fenton Ranch in Albuquerque, New Mexico; McKeever Environmental Learning Center, Sandy Lake, Pennsylvania; Pine Jog Environmental Education Center in West Palm Beach, Florida; The Schuylkill Center for Environmental Education in Philadelphia, Pennsylvania; Shaker Lakes Regional Nature Center, Cleveland, Ohio; and the Shaw Arboretum in Gray Summit, Missouri.

Future Plans

The Institute for Earth Education will continue to be a source of information for educators worldwide. The institute works on new information for students at all levels. One new project just begun is Earthlings. This program, just now in the development stages, will be for four- and five-year-olds.

Membership Information and Volunteer Possibilities

Annual membership in the Institute is $20, or $35 for professional members. Members receive *Talking Leaves*, the quarterly journal, and catalogs of materials and publications. All members receive a 10 percent discount on materials and publications as well as invitations to national and international conferences. Members will also receive a copy of *Seedbeds*, a listing of earth education job opportunities and upcoming workshops and events. *Heartwood* is also sent to members, reporting on the latest developments in earth education programs. A report of the international network of the institute is made to members through copies of *Branches*.

Volunteer possibilities are limited in the organization, since most of its work is in the publication of resource material. There are, however, a small number of people trained to lead workshops and teacher training programs.

☐ INTERNATIONAL COUNCIL FOR BIRD PRESERVATION

1250 24th Street, NW
Washington, DC 20037
or
801 Pennsylvania Avenue, SE
Washington, DC 20003
(202) 547-9009 or (202) 778-9563
Contact: Christopher Imboden, Executive Officer

History/Goals
International Council for Bird Preservation was established in 1922 by prominent American and European bird enthusiasts to work for the conservation of birds and their habitats. Today there are approximately 3,000 members, and ICBP has grown into a federation of over 300 member organizations representing some ten million people in 110 countries. ICBP works to protect endangered birds worldwide and to promote public awareness of the ecological importance of birds.

Past Achievements
The Council has expanded its network to 110 countries worldwide, including the developing tropical countries where few, if any, conservation movements existed prior to ICBP.

ICBP began a captive breeding program of pink pigeons, native to the island of Mauritius. In 1975 this species had dwindled to fewer than twenty birds. With ICBP's program, there are now over 100 birds that have been raised in captivity. Several pairs of the doves have been successfully released at the Botanic Gardens of Pamplemousses on Mauritius.

Ongoing Projects
ICBP is supporting efforts in southeastern Brazil to save the red-tailed parrot. ICBP is supporting a plan to turn an entire island into a refuge for the parrots, which exist only in a few isolated parts of Brazil.

ICBP purchased Cousin Island, famous for its seabirds, to save the Seychelles brush warbler. This warbler lives nowhere else in the world and had been reduced to only thirty birds before the council purchased the island. Today there are over 300 warblers, and ICBP continues to manage the island.

In Bali, the Rothschild's mynah finds its only home in the world. Fewer than 250 of these birds remain on Bali, and ICBP has begun studying the ecology of the bird and is trying to increase local interest in the mynah's welfare.

ICBP manages a computerized data bank that is constantly updated. ICBP compiles the international *Bird Red Data Book*, used by governments and conservationists worldwide.

Future Plans

ICBP, in an effort to protect the threatened habitat of the imperial Amazon parrot, has helped to purchase a forest reserve in Dominica, where there are only sixty of the parrots left. Through educational facilities and local interest, ICBP hopes to save the threatened bird. The council has also begun programs to stimulate wildlife tourism on the island, to provide a new source of income.

Membership Information and Volunteer Possibilities

Annual membership in ICBP is $35. Members receive the quarterly journal, *World Birdwatch*, as well as the *Bulletin*, published periodically to keep members up-to-date on conservation achievements. There are also occasional technical publications and ICBP study reports, which describe ongoing research and examine conservation issues in detail.

ICBP has a network of volunteers who share an interest in protecting the birds worldwide.

☐ INTERNATIONAL FUND FOR ANIMAL WELFARE

411 Main Street
P.O. Box 193
Yarmouth Port, MA 02675
(508) 362-4944
Contact: Brian Davies, Founder
Linda G. Porter, Administrative Assistant

History/Goals

The International Fund for Animal Welfare was founded in 1969 by Brian Davies in an attempt to end the killing of baby harp seals for their white coats by Norwegian and Canadian hunters in the Gulf of St. Lawrence. IFAW is a network of over 650,000 individual donor members throughout the world.

Past Achievements

In 1971 IFAW started Operation Bear-Lift to move polar bears away from Canadian towns they had been bothering. Eighty bears were moved to safety.

In 1978 IFAW worked to stop the killing of grey seals in Scotland.

In 1981 IFAW uncovered the extreme cruelty to dogs in the Philippines. Because of public outrage after IFAW's revelation, local laws were enacted in the Philippines in 1982 aimed at putting a stop to the cruelty and killing of dogs.

In 1985 IFAW helped establish the marine mammal sanctuary in Madeira, California.

In 1988 IFAW purchased a plot of land in Costa Rica, which was essential to save bees in that country.

After years of campaigning, 1989 brought a victory for IFAW when the European Community banned the importation of whitecoat and blueback seal skins.

Ongoing Projects

In 1987 IFAW began a campaign aimed at stopping the mass killing of millions of kangaroos in Australia. IFAW is taking on the Australian government in this campaign, attempting to force the government to change its kangaroo management plan that authorizes the killing of kangaroos each year in Australia.

In 1989 IFAW launched a campaign against cosmetics testing on animals. This is one of their major campaigns for the 1990s.

Future Plans

According to IFAW's report for the future, the organization, through public awareness and legislation, "will continue to promote and ensure the just and kind treatment of all animals everywhere. This means improving the quality of animals' lives and their environment, preserving them from extinction, and preventing and abolishing all cruelties done to them by humans."

IFAW plans to establish and operate an Australian branch office and will launch an educational campaign to increase public support for its programs.

Membership Information and Volunteer Possibilities

The International Fund for Animal Welfare does not charge a membership fee and does not set a minimum donation. The organization will recognize members after their donation by sending out approximately ten newsletters each year. The newsletter is designed to inform members about IFAW's progress and to call members to action to help in certain campaigns.

Members can volunteer to send in "action cards" to legislators and others, in the hopes of getting positive actions for IFAW's programs. There is also a Whale Stranding Network on Cape Cod for Massachusetts volunteers.

☐ INTERNATIONAL OCEANOGRAPHIC FOUNDATION

3979 Rickenbacker Causeway, Virginia Key
Miami, FL 33149–9900
(305) 361-5786 or 361-4888
Contact: Edward T. Foote II, President

History/Goals

The International Oceanographic Foundation was founded in 1953 by a board of trustees composed of scientists and laypersons devoted to the ocean. Today's members include divers, yacht owners, travelers, seafarers, educators, and scientists.

IOF was established to provide unbiased authoritative information to the public about the oceans of the world and their importance to people, and to encourage the scientific study of oceans. The foundation studies such things as fish, ocean currents, and the geology, chemistry, and physics of the sea and the sea floor.

Past Achievements

The International Oceanographic Foundation has grown into an organization with over 55,000 members in over ninety countries around the world. It has developed a permanent marine science museum in Florida that is visited by thousands of people each year.

Ongoing Projects

Each year IOF receives thousands of requests for information from around the world. The foundation handles each request individually, and each one is given a personal response.

Planet Ocean is a marine science show on permanent display in Florida. Each year this museum is visited by thousands of people, including teachers from all over Florida and sometimes from outside the state.

IOF arranges special expeditions for members to visit oceans around the world. These trips can range from whale watching in rubber rafts to luxury cruises in areas such as the China Sea, the Antarctic, the Galapagos Islands, and Easter Island.

Future Plans

IOF plans to expand the educational programs already in place. An educational kit is planned, based on the exhibits at Planet Ocean, which will be made available to teachers nationwide. There are also plans for traveling exhibits to visit museums across the country.

Membership Information and Volunteer Possibilities

Annual membership in IOF is $18. There are family memberships available for $25 and life memberships for $400. Membership is open to anyone with an interest in the oceans and a "desire to extend and develop vital research and exploration into them, to promote the collection and dissemination of scientific knowledge about them, and to encourage a program of research and education." Members receive the bimonthly *Sea Frontiers* magazine and the *Sea Secrets* bulletin. Members may purchase books from the Planet Ocean Book Shop at a special 10 percent discount.

Volunteers who go through a special IOF oceanographic course may work in the museum, guiding tours.

☐ INTERNATIONAL PRIMATE PROTECTION LEAGUE

P.O. Drawer 766
Summerville, SC 29484
(803) 871-7988
Contact: Shirley McGreal, Chairwoman and Founder

History/Goals
The International Primate Protection League was founded in 1973 by Shirley McGreal while she was living in Thailand. She was concerned with the capture, transport, and captive life of primates and has continued to work for the well-being of primates. IPPL has approximately 10,000 members and representatives in twenty-four countries. The advisory board for IPPL includes zoologists, anthropologists, medical doctors, biologists, veterinarians, and psychologists.

Past Achievements
In 1974 IPPL exposed a network of animal smugglers working between Thailand and the United States. After IPPL's exposure the network was closed down, saving the lives of hundreds of gibbon apes.

In 1975 IPPL organized Project Bangkok Airport. During this project, fifty college students worked in the Bangkok Airport noting the export conditions of primates from Thailand. When the resulting report was released, the public outcry was so great that a ban on the commercial exportation of all primates from Thailand was enacted.

An exposure in 1977 of the misuse of Rhesus monkeys for radiation experiments in the United States led to a ban by India on the exportation of all primates.

The "First Southeast Annual Exotic Animal Auction" was held in Atlanta, Georgia, in 1984. IPPL picketed the auction and no further auctions were held.

IPPL's long-term investigation into gorilla smuggling led, in 1990, to the arrest and jailing of West German wildlife smuggler Walter Sensen.

Ongoing Projects
IPPL is working on establishing patrols in Rwanda to protect the world's 200 remaining mountain gorillas from a recent series of poaching incidents.

IPPL's field representatives around the world work to help create national parks and sanctuaries and to strictly control the hunting, trapping, and sale of primates.

IPPL helps support a chimpanzee rehabilitation project in the Gambia, West Africa. This project is designed to help reintroduce once-captive chimpanzees back into the wild.

IPPL owns and manages a gibbon sanctuary in Summerville, South Carolina. At the sanctuary IPPL currently supports eighteen gibbons at a cost of approximately $45,000 annually.

Future Plans
IPPL is planning on an expansion of several enclosures at the gibbon sanctuary in South Carolina. There are also plans for an indoor/outdoor housing unit for the gorillas.

IPPL is also working on a permanent ban on the importation of wild-caught primates to the United States.

Membership Information and Volunteer Possibilities
Annual membership in the International Primate Protection League is $20. There are reduced student/hardship memberships available for $10 per year. Members receive a quarterly subscription to the IPPL *Newsletter*. There are no formal volunteer programs available.

☐ THE IZAAK WALTON LEAGUE OF AMERICA
1401 Wilson Boulevard, Level B
Arlington, VA 22209
(703) 528-1818
Contact: Jack Lorenz, Executive Director

History/Goals
The Izaak Walton League was founded in 1922 to protect the nation's soil, air, woods, water, and wildlife. Today there are over 50,000 members and more than 400 local chapters nationwide.

The Izaak Walton League fights for clean water, clean air, wildlife habitat, public land management, farm conservation, protection of natural areas, and enhanced outdoor recreation. The league meets these goals by promoting citizen involvement; educating the public about threats to the environment; representing conservation issues before Congress, state legislatures, and government agencies; and by enforcing the regulations through court actions.

Past Achievements
In 1969 the league started the Save Our Streams (SOS) program as a grassroots water-quality monitoring program. There are now 200 chapters and over 600 local stream projects involved in the SOS program. In 1988 the program published *A Citizen's Directory for Water Quality Abuses*, along with a stream adoption kit and other educational resources aimed at both children and adults.

Also in 1988 the league coauthored the soil and agricultural sections of the Blueprint for the Environment, a national agenda that was given to the incoming Bush administration. The league has also written testimony, which was presented in 1988 to the U.S. Senate Agriculture Subcommittee on Research, Conservation, and Forestry concerning conservation provisions of the Farm Act.

In 1987 The Izaac Walton League purchased a $700,000 helicopter for federal law enforcement officers to use against poachers in the Gulf Coast marshes.

Ongoing Projects

Since 1977 the league's outdoor ethics program has worked to reduce poaching, trespassing, and other illegal outdoor activities. The program also encourages hunter education.

The league has several major ongoing projects: the Chesapeake Bay regional program, which promotes the restoration of the bay through public education, public policy, and local wetland and stream development; the Ohio River watershed protection project, which works through Save Our Streams and involves over 6,000 individuals and 400 groups, chapters, and schools; the Upper Mississippi River regional program, which concentrates on groundwater contamination, soil erosion and farm conservation, waterfowl management, acid rain and clean air issues, and the protection of fish and other wildlife in the Mississippi River; and the public lands restoration task force, which works on finding a balance between the competing uses of western public forests and rangelands and their water, fish, and wildlife.

The league has been producing a weekly half-hour public affairs television show for over fifteen years. The show presents current topics of interest concerning the national and international environment and is seen by millions of viewers via satellite and cable television.

The IWLA Endowment is an affiliate of the league that purchases and protects critical natural areas throughout the United States.

In 1982 the league received a grant from the Richard King Mellon Foundation for the express purpose of expanding the league's hunter ethics program. IWLA has developed a clearinghouse for outdoor and hunter ethics information.

Various chapters throughout the country have ongoing projects. The Santa Ana, California, chapter, in conjunction with the California Bureau of Land Management, conducts desert awareness campouts. These campouts are used to teach participants about the wildlife and vegetation in the desert ecosystem.

The Mossy Creek and Bill Kieffer/Lakeway chapters in Tennessee have been working with an alliance of conservation groups to force Champion International Paper Corporation to clean up the Pigeon River. The corporation has agreed to invest $100 million to update its plant to meet federal and state water quality standards. IWLA is continuing to work on the current water quality and on cleanup plans.

Future Plans

The league is working to build the National Conservation Center and national headquarters on the IWLA's conservation park in Gaithersburg, Maryland. This park, just north of Washington, D.C., will be open to visitors and will serve as a demonstration center for energy and natural resource conservation techniques.

The league recently began a national youth conservation education program called Uncle Ike. IWLA would like to see an Uncle Ike program set up in all 100 league chapters nationwide. This program is designed to teach children about conservation and provide them with the necessary basis for conservation measures in the future.

Membership Information and Volunteer Possibilities

Annual membership in the Izaak Walton League of America is $20. There are student memberships available for only $5 and family memberships for $30. There are also $250 lifetime memberships. Members of IWLA receive a subscription to *Outdoor America*, the quarterly magazine, as well as membership in the IWLA Endowment and special deals on life and health insurance and car rentals.

League members are eligible to join the Action Network. Activist members receive special reports on legislative developments as well as action alerts. Members of the league can become involved at many levels. The Save Our Streams program is a volunteer program working on specific stream projects. *Splash*, the SOS newsletter, keeps those involved with the program in touch and informed.

The public lands restoration task force has developed riparian enhancement teams. These volunteers help ranchers build fences to keep cattle out of riparian zones.

The wetlands watch program is also a volunteer network of citizens and local groups who are taught to identify and protect wetlands areas in their local communities. A wetlands watch kit has been developed and includes a fact sheet on wetlands, pertinent legislation, a fact sheet for schoolchildren, and a resource list of further information.

☐ THE JANE GOODALL INSTITUTE FOR WILDLIFE RESEARCH, EDUCATION, AND CONSERVATION

P.O. Box 41720
Tucson, AZ 85717
(602) 325-1211
Contacts: Robert J. Edison, Chief Operating Officer and Director of Development and Public Affairs
Michael D. Aisner, Media Liaison and Special Projects
Jennifer Kenyon, Administrative Assistant

History/Goals

The Jane Goodall Institute was founded by Dr. Jane Goodall, who began working with the chimpanzees over thirty years ago, to provide research on wild chimpanzees and to study captive chimpanzees. The institute's goal is to protect, conserve, and see to the well-being of wild and captive chimpanzees.

There are currently 2,314 members in the organization, and offices in the United States, the United Kingdom, Canada, and Tanzania.

Past Achievements

In September 1990 Dr. Goodall published *Through a Window: My Thirty Years with the Chimpanzees of Gombe,* the long-awaited sequel to *In the Shadow of Man.*

In March 1989 Dr. Goodall met in Burundi with the American Ambassador and the president, the secretary general and numerous other ministers and officials of Burundi. The groups discussed the conservation of the chimpanzee population in Burundi and how to develop controlled tourism to foster economic growth. As a result of these talks, JGI-UK sponsored a student to travel to Burundi to begin the study of a group of chimpanzees in the southern part of the country.

A sanctuary titled Monkey World was created in Dorset, England, to house unwanted and/or abused primates. This sanctuary provides a safe haven for chimpanzees rescued from such situations as the beach photographers in Spain who use sedated young chimpanzees to attract clients.

Since 1988 JGI has participated in a series of international workshops to discuss the use of chimpanzees by biomedical research facilities. Individuals from a broad range of interests, including lab directors, veterinarians, research scientists, and animal welfare activists, are invited to attend. The workshops include discussions and some helpful recommendations.

In March of 1990 the Jane Goodall Institute, in cooperation with the World Wildlife Fund and the Humane Society of the United States, obtained a ruling that reclassified the chimpanzee as an endangered species under the U.S. Endangered Species Act.

Ongoing Projects

Many of the programs of JGI are ongoing, including the administration of Monkey World, work in Burundi, field research, workshops, and television programs. In particular, there is a ChimpanZoo program involving fifteen zoos throughout the United States. A computer program is being put together by a panel of scientific advisors that will make it possible for researchers to correlate data collected at different sites. A ChimpanZoo newsletter was just begun in 1990 and is available to members, detailing further activities of this program.

Future Plans

The Jane Goodall Institute, in cooperation with the government of Burundi, is planning on establishing a sanctuary for chimpanzees. This sanctuary, made possible in part by a donation from actress Kirstie Alley, is being built by the designer of Monkey World. Educational facilities are also planned at the site, to help educate tourists and the local population on the importance of preserving the chimpanzees and their habitat.

JGI is also working with the chairman of its Committee for the Conservation and Care of Chimpanzees in Africa to establish a conservation plan to be used throughout the chimpanzees' range in Africa. The plan would be used as a basis for all projects involving the chimpanzees in Africa and would supplement plans already submitted by the U.S. Fish and Wildlife Service to aid the chimpanzees. The committee is also working with TRAFFIC USA, a JGI program, to bring attention to the international chimpanzee trade and the need to keep better track of the trade to curtail illegal activity.

Membership Information and Volunteer Possibilities

Basic membership in the Jane Goodall Institute is $25 annually. Members receive quarterly reports: three *JGI International Bulletins* and one *Membership Report* at the end of the year.

Fellowships are available to college students through the University of Southern California Goodall Fellowship. College students participate in various studies worldwide.

☐ LEAGUE OF CONSERVATION VOTERS

1150 Connecticut Avenue, NW, Suite 201
Washington, DC 20036
(202) 785-8683
Contacts: Jim Maddy, Executive Director
Donna J. Greenberg, Administrative Assistant

History/Goals

The League of Conservation Voters was established in 1970 by Marion Edey, a House committee staffer. The League is an unaffiliated political action committee working to find, support, and elect candidates to federal office who favor protecting the nation's environment. Support is given through financial contributions, campaign staff support, and public endorsements. The league's twenty-four-member board of directors is composed of leaders from environmental organizations who volunteer their time to work with the league.

The league currently has no formal members but approximately 15,000 active supporters. There are no local chapters of LCV, but there are twelve independent state organizations that cooperate closely with LCV, such as the California League of Conservation Voters.

Past Achievements

During the 1990 elections LCV produced two television ads. "Greenscam" was one advertisement that was run when an opponent to an LCV-backed candidate tried to convince the public that he or she was an environmentalist or tried to distort the record of the LCV-backed candidate. The other commercial, "Decisions," was a positive endorsement for a candidate supported by LCV.

In 1986 the League contributed close to $100,000 to candidates for various federal offices. Seven new pro-environment senators were elected with the help of LCV: senators Wirth (D-Colo.); Graham (D-Fla.); Fowler (D-Ga.); Mikulski (D-Md.); Reid (D-Nev.); Conrad (D-N.Dak.); and Daschle (D-S.Dak.).

In 1988, 79 percent of the seventy-six House and Senate candidates backed by LCV won reelection. In 1990 the league endorsed over 100 candidates and doubled the money it spent on endorsements from the 1988 election.

Ongoing Projects

The league provides support to campaign staffs in several different ways: placing LCV field organizers on campaign staffs; production of advertisements and paying for and placing the ads on radio and television; and the production of literature that endorses the candidate.

The league publishes the *National Environmental Scorecard*, a record on the votes cast by members of Congress concerning various environmental issues. The *Scorecard* also rates House and Senate members according to their environmental votes.

Future Plans

The League of Conservation Voters will continue to serve as the political arm of America's environmental movement. The 1992 elections will be another big challenge for the league, and they will work to let the public know how members of Congress and presidential candidates stand on environmental issues.

Membership Information and Volunteer Possibilities

There is no formal membership in LCV, but with a $25 donation "members" can receive the *National Environmental Scorecard*, along with other special publications. The *Scorecard* is also available to nonmembers for $5.

There are summer internships available with the league. LCV also helps recruit volunteers to staff campaign offices of endorsed candidates.

☐ LIGHTHAWK

P.O. Box 8163
Santa Fe, NM 87504–8163
(505) 982-9656
Contact: Michael Stewartt, Executive Director

History/Goals

LightHawk was originally begun in 1974 as Project LightHawk. In full-time operation since 1980, the organization officially shortened its name in 1989 to LightHawk. LightHawk was founded for educational and scientific purposes. Specifically, the organization provides airborne transportation and other flight assistance to conservation organizations. Since its founding, LightHawk has flown thousands of missions for over 100 environmental organizations.

LightHawk's primary goal is to educate people through the media about the environment. This is often accomplished by flying legislators and conservationists over clear-cut areas. LightHawk helps the environmental movement through grassroots organizing, aerial surveys and photographs, expanded media exposure, and rapid transportation of those seeking to make a difference.

Past Achievements

A 1988 LightHawk flight with Colorado's Senator Tim Wirth over Piñon Canyon in southeastern Colorado led, in 1990, to Senate approval of an amendment to protect the canyon and the Purgatoire River valley. The amendment transfers 16,700 acres in the canyon from the U.S. Army to the U.S. Forest Service, and stipulates that no activity is allowed in the canyon that would impair the preservation of the paleontological, archeological, and natural resources of the area.

In early 1990 LightHawk convinced the government of Belize to establish the 97,000-acre Bladen Nature Reserve in an area of Belize threatened by logging. This preserve is larger than all of the other parks and reserves in Belize combined.

In 1990 LightHawk received the National Wildlife Federation's National Conservation Achievement Award for "outstanding contributions to the wise use and management of the nation's natural resources."

Ongoing Projects

In addition to providing flights over threatened areas, LightHawk conducts surveys of remote habitat and locates grizzly bears, bobcats, trumpeter swans, wolves, or other rare species, saving months of fieldwork.

LightHawk's operations are supported by two Cessna Turbo-210s. LightHawk's executive director and chief pilot has flown over 7,000 hours in the western United States and as a bush pilot in Alaska.

LightHawk has published an eight-minute videotape entitled "The Ancient Forests, A Call to Action." The tape, documenting the plight of the forests in the Pacific Northwest, features Dennis Weaver and is available for $14.

Future Plans

In 1988 LightHawk expanded its services into Central America. LightHawk will continue to bring its services to the environmental cause in the United States and will take those same techniques to Central America as funds are made available.

Membership Information and Volunteer Possibilities

Annual membership in LightHawk is $35. Members receive a subscription to the quarterly newsletter, *LightHawk: The Wings of Conservation.*

LightHawk recruits the services of aircraft owners and pilots. Light-Hawk encourages these people to coordinate some volunteer time with LightHawk to help fill the organization's needs for pilots and additional aircraft.

☐ MANOMET BIRD OBSERVATORY
P.O. Box 936
Manomet, MA 02345
(508) 224-6521
Contacts: Linda E. Leddy, President and Director
Nancy W. Axelson, Membership/Development
Assistant

History/Goals
The Manomet Bird Observatory was founded in 1969 to carry out long-term research and educational programs in environmental biology. MBO program's help researchers understand wildlife populations and natural systems. There are two educational programs, one to provide college students with a semester of field experience and the other to provide support to science educators in the school systems. There are currently 2,500 members in the organization.

Past Achievements
Since its founding, MBO biologists have captured, measured, and released over 200,000 birds and have spent a decade surveying whale and seabird habitats along the continental shelf.

During 1988–89, the tropical forest program project director, Nicholas V. L. Brokaw, analyzed conservation and forestry practices in Belize with a team of foresters and economists from around the world. The international team then made recommendations for the Belize government.

In 1985 the Western Hemisphere Shorebird Reserve Network (WHSRN) was launched by MBO and the National Audubon Society. This volunteer network united governmental wildlife agencies and conservation groups in eleven countries in an effort to develop a sustainable management and conservation plan of wetlands around the world. In 1988 WHSRN developed the *Field Manual for Studying and Handling Shorebirds*. This manual has since been translated into Spanish and Portuguese and will be used as a research guideline for fieldwork in Latin America.

Ongoing Projects
MBO operates a research site on Quebec's Gaspé Peninsula. Studies have looked at such things as how the forest structure affects physical characteristics or warbler song, and documenting changes in the abundance of breeding warbler species.

The tropical forest program has an ongoing bird survey program in the Rio Bravo Conservation Area in Belize. The program also works with the Belizeans to train them in field research techniques.

MBO began hosting tours to coastal Belize in 1990. This program allows MBO members to visit Belize with trained researchers to view projects and see the various habitats in that country.

The MBO domestic sea sampling program works with the fishing industry by sending sea samplers on commercial fishing boats during normal fishing trips. The samplers travel only on those vessels whose captains volunteer to have them, and use the time to identify and classify the catch. This provides important data for fisheries conservation and management. The program has also provided a valuable network to fishermen by providing them fishery regulations and even alerting vessels to imminent dangers such as undersea telephone cables.

The environmental education program offers programs and curriculum materials for schoolchildren and their teachers, in an effort to improve science studies. The program has joined efforts with the Museum Institute for Teaching, a consortium of seven museums funded by the National Science Foundation, to provide teacher workshops and consultants.

The field biology training program was developed in 1985 as a way to provide college and graduate students with field experience necessary for their science studies. Students from over thirty colleges have participated in the program since its inception.

Future Plans

MBO studies wildlife and habitats from Canada to southern Argentina and will continue these studies into the future. College students will continue to participate in the field research training program. Plans are underway to expand school programs and curriculum materials for teachers in the elementary and secondary schools.

Membership Information and Volunteer Possibilities

Annual membership in Manomet Bird Observatory is $25. There are reduced memberships for students and seniors available at $15 annually. Members receive a subscription to the newsletter, a copy of the annual report, and notice of special events, and are eligible to participate in field trips at special rates.

College students can volunteer to participate in the field training program and receive college credit for the semester they spend doing research. Members can also participate in field trips and educational programs that concentrate on MBO's research programs. There is also a shorebird survey in which volunteers assist researchers in collecting data from captured birds, which are later released.

☐ MISSION: WOLF

P.O. Box 211
Silver Cliff, CO 81249
(719) 746-2919
Contacts: Kent Weber

History/Goals
Mission: Wolf was established as a refuge for wolves. Located on over thirty-six acres in Colorado's Sangre de Cristo mountains, the sanctuary is currently home to ten wolves and twenty wolf-dogs.

Past Achievements
The wolves currently living in the natural enclosures at the sanctuary were received from a variety of unpleasant situations. Some are from people who wanted to own wolves as "pets"; others come from roadside zoos or from breeders who were unable to place the wolves in private homes. One of the wolves was rescued from a fur farm.

Ongoing Projects
Mission: Wolf uses the wolves as an educational tool to help the public and, in particular, schoolchildren, across the United States understand wolves better. The "ambassador wolf" is Shaman, a black Canadian timberwolf. Shaman travels across the country and visits schools, clubs, nature centers, and other interested groups. The film *Death of a Legend* accompanies Shaman on his visits. Mission: Wolf requests a $250 donation from any group requesting the traveling wolf program to help offset costs of the program. During 1990 over 200,000 schoolchildren were reached through the educational outreach program.

Another educational aspect of the sanctuary is that visitors are welcome to visit the sanctuary at any time throughout the year. The sanctuary is accessible year-round, but there is no running water through the winter. There are a limited number of indoor sleeping quarters, so visitors are asked to come prepared to camp outdoors. Visitors must provide their own food, water, and beverages and are reminded that there is no indoor plumbing at the sanctuary.

Future Plans
The thirty-six-acre sanctuary is adjacent to 385 acres of private land on three sides, which Mission: Wolf would like to purchase in the future to expand the sanctuary.

Mission: Wolf is also hoping to build an education center at the refuge in the future. The construction of the center proceeds only as materials become available through donations of either materials or money.

Membership Information and Volunteer Possibilities
There is no formal membership in Mission: Wolf; rather, there is an adoption plan in which adoption fees are utilized to provide the care of the wolves. Students can adopt for $25, individuals for $40, and families

or groups for $100. Each "foster parent" receives a color photograph of the adopted wolf, a certificate of adoption, and a description of the wolf's personality. When the wolf sheds in the spring, the adoptive parent will receive a piece of the wolf's fur. This adoption entitles the foster parent to a one-year subscription to *Wolf Visions*, the quarterly newsletter. Admittance to the sanctuary is also included in the annual adoption fee. The organization also takes donations of materials in lieu of cash for the adoption fee.

Volunteers are utilized frequently at the sanctuary. Volunteers help coordinate the newsletter, are helping to do the construction work on the education center, and are asked to help with donations for both the sanctuary and the traveling education program.

☐ THE NATIONAL ARBOR DAY FOUNDATION
100 Arbor Avenue
Nebraska, City, NE 68410
(402) 474-5655
Contacts: John Rosenow, Executive Director
Joan Giannola, Members Services

History/Goals
J. Sterling Morton helped establish the holiday called Arbor Day to commemorate the lasting beauty of trees. From this holiday grew The National Arbor Day Foundation, established in 1972. Today there are over 800,000 members of the foundation throughout the United States, all working to provide the knowledge and skill necessary to make informed decisions to children and adults alike. The programs of The National Arbor Day Foundation are used by city and state officials, foresters, citizen volunteers, teachers, television and radio stations, magazines, soil conservation districts, and farmers to help further the cause of conservation and tree planting at the local and national levels.

Past Achievements
During 1988 and 1989 the foundation ran a successful television and radio campaign entitled "Plant Trees to Fight the Greenhouse Effect." The public service announcements were narrated by Eddie Albert, and printed copies of the ads were sent to newspapers and magazines across the country.

The foundation has established a network of Tree City USAs across the country. These cities received this designation because of their dedication to tree planting and conservation measures. During 1988–89 the foundation certified a record 1053 Tree City USAs in forty-seven states and the District of Columbia.

Ongoing Projects
The National Arbor Day Foundation has four major ongoing projects: Conservation Trees program, Tree City USA, Trees for America, and

Celebrate Arbor Day. The Conservation Trees program teaches Americans about the importance of trees to the conservation of the soil, energy, water, wildlife, and the atmosphere. To date, 1,300,000 copies of the *Conservation Trees* booklets have been distributed across the United States, showing readers how to use shade trees and windbreaks in energy conservation, how to save trees during home construction, how to increase farm profits, how to prune trees, and other useful information.

The Tree City USA program recognizes urban and community forestry programs and provides technical assistance, public awareness, and other support for the programs. The Friends of Tree City USA project seeks to involve civic leaders and individuals in tree care and programs. The *Tree City USA Bulletin* provides members and leaders with the latest information from the foundation.

The Trees for America program is a stewardship program designed to encourage each citizen to plant a tree. To date the foundation has distributed over seven million trees to hundreds of thousands of Americans, along with over one million copies of *The Tree Book*. *The Tree Book* contains photos to be used in identification, steps to tree planting, information about pruning, hardiness zone maps, and information on fruit- and nut-bearing trees.

The Celebrate Arbor Day! program is a national program designed to recognize good stewards and to educate tomorrow's good stewards. The foundation's education units have been distributed to thousands of schools throughout the country. The "Grow Your Own Tree" program is for kindergarten through third grade, and the "Trees are Terrific" program is for fifth graders. Both units give students the firsthand experience of caring for trees.

An Arbor Day catalog has been published with merchandise and books designed to promote tree planting. A how-to book for those planning Arbor Day celebrations in local communities has been distributed nationwide.

Future Plans

The National Arbor Day Foundation is developing an education and conference facility at the National Arbor Day Center in Nebraska City, Nebraska. J. Sterling Morton's agricultural estate is the home of the center, and the educational facility will house the continuing education program, a professional development center, and conference programs.

The foundation is committed to helping provide practical environmental education to Americans well into the future.

Membership Information and Volunteer Possibilities

Annual membership in the National Arbor Day Foundation is $10. Members receive the bimonthly magazine, *Arbor Day*, which keeps them informed about ongoing programs. The foundation also sponsors member weekends in which members from across the country gather at the center in Nebraska to share in a program on stewardship, education, and recreation.

Volunteers are used at the local level to promote trees and tree conservation and to encourage community involvement in programs.

☐ NATIONAL AUDUBON SOCIETY

950 Third Avenue
New York, NY 10022
(212) 832–3200
Contact: Peter A. A. Berle, President

History/Goals
The National Audubon Society was founded in 1905, when thirty-five protest groups incorporated to oppose the killing of plumed birds for use in women's hats. Originally the National Association of Audubon Societies for the Protection of Wild Birds and Animals, the organization has always been concerned with the conservation of birds and their habitat. Today, the organization has broadened its range of concern to include all wildlife. NAS calls itself the "voice of reason" and focuses on a wide range of conservation topics, including the conservation of plants and animals and their habitats, land and water use, energy policies, pollution, and global environmental problems.

The National Audubon Society today has over 500,000 members, with the support of nine regional offices, five state offices, and over 500 local chapters throughout the United States. There are numerous Audubon societies throughout the United States that are independent and not affiliated with the National Audubon Society. NAS operates sanctuaries, conducts research, lobbies Congress, and encourages a broad spectrum of educational programs.

Past Achievements
The National Audubon Society has acquired land throughout the United States that is maintained as wildlife sanctuaries. NAS has succeeded in providing refuge to such species as the pronghorn antelope, pintail ducks, marshweed owls, and spotted owls.

Audubon has become a respected resource for those seeking information on environmental issues. The society has sponsored scientific conferences, workshops, and seminars on various wildlife and environmental topics.

Ongoing Projects
The National Audubon Society is currently conducting research on topics ranging from whooping crane behavior to the effects of energy exploration on wildlife. Seminars on grizzly bears are conducted and there is a long-standing reward for information about the illegal killing of grizzly bears.

Audubon currently manages eighty-two wildlife sanctuaries in the United States. In one of its most popular programs, Audubon takes environmental issues into classrooms. The Audubon Adventure Clubs are active in over 7,000 U.S. elementary school classrooms, and travel study programs are arranged for high school and college students.

An annual reference, *Audubon Wildlife Report*, is a guide to the country's wildlife management programs, and Audubon specials are seen regularly on Public Broadcasting Service (PBS) and SuperStation TBS.

Future Plans

The National Audubon Society plans to continue its programs of research, education, lobbying, and preservation into the future. A group of government relations experts in Washington, D.C., help to fight for Society-sponsored and backed bills. The role of the wildlife preservation program is expected to increase as civilization encroaches more and more on wetlands, forests, and other wilderness areas. Audubon hopes to help protect thousands of additional species under its preservation programs.

Audubon hopes to continue educating the public through its publications, films, programs at education centers and camps, and the Audubon Adventures program.

Membership Information and Volunteer Possibilities

Annual membership in the National Audubon Society is $30 and includes a subscription to the bimonthly magazine, *Audubon*, membership in one of the local Audubon chapters, admission to Audubon nature centers and sanctuaries, invitations to the ecology camps and workshops, the opportunity to participate in Audubon tours, and discounts on nature books and gifts.

There are a variety of volunteer opportunities in Audubon. There is an annual Christmas bird count in which members help collect data nationwide utilized by the Audubon researchers. Members are encouraged to help organize and participate in community projects, letter writing, and lobbying.

For an annual fee of $9, in addition to membership fees, an Audubon member may become a member of the Audubon Activist Network. As an activist the member will receive the bimonthly newsjournal *Audubon Activist* and "action alerts" to keep posted on congressional developments.

The Citizens' Acid Rain Monitoring Network encourages members to test and report on the acidity of rainfall across the country.

The one- and two-week ecology camps and workshops are offered to members at Audubon camps in Connecticut, Maine, and Wyoming. These camps allow members to experience nature firsthand and enjoy the natural world Audubon works to preserve.

Audubon tours are sponsored to destinations around the globe to help educate the public and illustrate some of the variety of wildlife and habitats worldwide.

☐ NATIONAL COALITION AGAINST THE MISUSE OF PESTICIDES

530 Seventh Street, SE
Washington, DC 20003
(202) 543–5450
Contacts: Jay Feldman, National Coordinator
Barbara Wetmore, Administrative Assistant

History/Goals
The National Coalition Against the Misuse of Pesticides was established in 1981 to focus on the public health, environmental, and economic problems of pesticide use. NCAMP is a coalition of health, environmental, labor, farm, consumer, and church groups, along with individuals concerned about the potential hazards of pesticides.

Past Achievements
In the decade since its founding, NCAMP has established itself as a network designed to address pesticide safety and safer alternatives to pesticide use.

Ongoing Projects
NCAMP is a clearinghouse of information for the concerned public and operates a 2,000-volume library. NCAMP can provide information on chemicals, pest control, and pesticide issues such as the use of pesticides in schools and on golf courses. NCAMP keeps members up-to-date on developments in the Federal Insecticide, Fungicide and Rodenticide Act (FIFRA).

NCAMP supports scientific research and review of pesticides and pesticide exposure. NCAMP also helps organize community projects designed to promote alternative forms of pest management.

Annually, NCAMP offers seed grants to help local groups working on controlling pesticide use and promoting alternatives.

There are a wide range of individuals who belong to NCAMP, such as pesticide "victims," farmers, farmworkers, gardeners, consumers, toxicologists, researchers, former chemical company scientists, state and federal regulators, physicians, and attorneys. These people work together to bring the issues out to the public and to combat the chemical industry.

NCAMP also publishes a wide range of materials on pesticide issues. Brochures, available for fifty cents each, cover issues such as pesticide safety, alternative pest control, pest control for fruits and vegetables. Booklets, ranging in price from $2 to $10, cover such topics as water safety, lawn maintenance, and a series of chemical profiles known as

Pesticide Reviews. These reviews give an in-depth chemical profile along with health and environmental effects and alternatives. Other publications include technical reports, summaries of state and local pesticide ordinances, pest control fact sheets, a library aid for students, and a "how-to" series.

Future Plans

The National Coalition Against the Misuse of Pesticides plans to continue its public awareness campaigns designed to bring the issues of pesticide dangers and alternatives to the public's attention.

Membership Information and Volunteer Possibilities

Annual membership in NCAMP is $20, with special rates for low income individuals. Members receive a copy of the CAMP newsletter, *Pesticides and You*. Members can also subscribe to *NCAMP's Technical Report*, a monthly news bulletin available for an additional $20 annually.

Volunteers are encouraged to work at the local level to make citizens aware of the dangers of pesticides and the possible alternatives, and NCAMP is available to offer assistance if necessary. Because of NCAMP's unique position as a network of organizations, it can offer guidance to members who want to become involved at the local level by directing them to local offices of organizations who work actively in pesticide issues.

☐ NATIONAL COALITION TO STOP FOOD IRRADIATION

P.O. Box 59–0488
San Francisco, CA 94159
(415) 626–2734
Contact: Mary Carol Randall, Administrator

History/Goals

The National Coalition to Stop Food Irradiation was established in 1984 to address the increasing threat of food irradiation. NCSFI is a coalition of over ninety affiliated groups and organizations around the world, working to protest food irradiation, to educate the public on the issues of food irradiation, and to provide information to individuals and groups. While NCSFI is an information clearinghouse and a distribution center supporting the fight against food irradiation, it is allied with Food and Water, Inc., in New York, which plays the activist role for the network.

Past Achievements

The coalition and Food and Water, Inc., produced a forty-minute videocassette on radiation-exposed food. The film, which gives an overview of irradiation and the status of regulations and technology around the world, has been used for conferences, educational talks, and activist training. It is available for $15.

NCSFI has published a 240-page *Information Manual*. The manual, contained in a three-ring notebook, includes scientific studies, articles, fact sheets, and press clippings. This manual is ideal for community organizers and activists.

Ongoing Projects
NCSFI is an information clearinghouse and continues to publish and distribute information concerning food irradiation. NCSFI networks information every two months to activist organizations around the world.

NCSFI has an ongoing adopt-a-library program in which individuals can adopt a library by sending $15 to NCSFI along with the name and address of a library. For the $15, NCSFI will send the designated library a year's subscription to *Food Irradiation Alert*, NCSFI's quarterly newsletter.

Future Plans
NCSFI will continue to serve as an information clearinghouse and to distribute information to various activist organizations.

Membership Information and Volunteer Possibilities
Annual membership in NCSFI is $25. Low-income memberships are available for $15. Members receive a year's subscription to *Food Irradiation Alert*.

NCSFI serves as a clearinghouse for information and can offer assistance and information to those volunteering at the local level. Actual volunteer opportunities are available through Food and Water, Inc., which offers volunteers the opportunity to organize local groups and work on the front lines of the grassroots movement.

☐ NATIONAL INSTITUTE FOR URBAN WILDLIFE
10921 Trotting Ridge Way
Columbia, MD 21044
(301) 596–3311
Contact: Gomer E. Jones, President

History/Goals
The National Institute for Urban Wildlife was founded in 1973 as a scientific and educational organization dealing with fish and wildlife in urban and suburban areas. The institute advocates the enhancement of urban wildlife values and habitat.

The institute works to provide information and the methodologies necessary to manage and enjoy wildlife and wildlife habitats in urban areas. It accomplishes this goal in three ways: by conducting research on the relationship between man and wildlife in an urban setting; by discovering and publicizing procedures for maintaining, enhancing, or controlling wildlife species in urban settings; and by increasing the public's appreciation for wildlife and the environment.

Past Achievements

The institute's research has resulted in the publication of numerous reports, including: *Planning for Wildlife in Cities and Suburbs; Urban Wetlands for Stormwater Control and Wildlife Enhancement; Planning for Urban Fishing and Waterfront Recreation; Highway-Wildlife Relationships: A State-of-the-Art Report;* and *An Annotated Bibliography on Planning and Management for Urban-Suburban Wildlife.*

The institute has studied the effects of urbanization on wildlife as well as the effects on wildlife of such things as building designs, stream channelization, military installations, and open space and recreation sites. This research has led to such publications as: *Compatibility of Fish, Wildlife, and Floral Resources with Electric Power Facilities; Environmental Conservation and the Petroleum Industry;* and *Environmental Reclamation and the Coal Surface Mining Industry.*

Ongoing Projects

The institute has four basic programs: research, urban conservation education, technical services, and urban wildlife sanctuaries. The institute's research has focused primarily on the relationship between man and wildlife in urban settings. The research has been designed for government, industry, developers, planners, engineers, students, and the general public.

The urban conservation education program aims to provide usable information for professional and nonprofessionals alike concerning major issues on urban wildlife. The educational program has resulted in the publication of documents such as *A Guide to Urban Wildlife Management;* the *Wildlife Habitat Conservation Teacher's* PAC series; the *Urban Wildlife Manager's Notebook* series; and various reports, guides, conferences, and seminars.

The technical services program provides information and services to urban planners and developers, land managers, state and federal non-game programs, and homeowners. The institute provides environmental assessments and impact statements; open space planning and management; aquatic space planning and management; recreational planning; experimental design; urban wetlands enhancement; terrestrial and aquatic field research; data analysis; literature research; environmental education and training; expert testimony; and natural resources management on corporate and public lands.

The urban wildlife sanctuaries program is working to certify a network of sanctuaries on private and public land throughout the United States. The program is designed to recognize landowners who dedicate their property to wildlife. Upon certification, the institute's staff of wildlife biologists will be made available to the landowner to answer questions and for consultations.

Future Plans

The institute will continue with its current programs. More land is sought throughout the country for inclusion in the national roster of urban wildlife sanctuaries and for certification by the institute. Research programs will continue, and the institute will continue to publish information concerning its research.

Membership Information and Volunteer Possibilities

Annual membership in the National Institute for Urban Wildlife is a minimum of $25. Members receive a year's subscription to the quarterly *Urban Wildlife News* and the quarterly how-to series, *Urban Wildlife Manager's Notebook*. Members also receive a 10 percent discount on institute publications, a 20 percent discount on institute activity fees, and invitations to all institute activities and programs. There is a "hot line" number available to members in which free advice and consultations can be received from the staff of urban wildlife biologists.

Although there are no formal volunteer programs within the institute, the institute does provide counsel to those working at the grassroots level. There are also numerous institute activities and programs offered to members.

☐ NATIONAL PARKS AND CONSERVATION ASSOCIATION

1015 Thirty-first Street, NW
Washington, DC 20007
(202) 944–8530
Contacts: Paul C. Pritchard, President
　　　　　Laura Loomis, Director of Grassroots and
　　　　　　　Outreach
　　　　　Terry L. Vines, Director of Membership

History/Goals

The National Parks and Conservation Association was established in 1919 to defend, promote, and improve the U.S. National Park System and to educate the public about parks and conservation.

There are currently over 100,000 members in NPCA.

Past Achievements

NPCA helped expand the boundaries of several existing parks throughout the United States, including the Congaree Swamp, Big Cypress, Everglades, the Manassas Battlefield, Harpers Ferry, Antietam, and Salem Maritime. NPCA has also helped establish several new parks in the past few years, including the San Francisco Maritime, Charles Pinckney, Natchez, and Zuni-Cibola historical areas.

NPCA worked with Friends of Gateway to block a theme park and other development at Gateway National Recreation Area near New York City.

NPCA and scientists from the University of Maryland and Penn State analyzed visitor impacts at parks and developed a plan for managing the impacts. The report is available for land managers and others interested in the study.

Ongoing Projects

NPCA has established a $1 million revolving fund that is used for land acquisitions. Many of the lands acquired by NPCA are donated to the National Park Service for inclusion in the U.S. park system.

NPCA has an ongoing education program. Through its education center, NPCA offers books, videos, and guides. NPCA has developed a fourth- through sixth-grade curriculum plan to educate students on endangered species, biodiversity, and habitat.

NPCA continually works to increase the national park system by extending boundaries or acquiring new lands. One of the ongoing projects is the continued protection of Manassas National Battlefield Park.

Future Plans

National Parks and Conservation Association continues to focus on defending and improving the national park system within the United States. One of the major focuses in the future is education of the public. NPCA will continue to lobby Congress to support its proposals and will continue to work on land acquisitions and increasing the sizes of current parks.

Membership Information and Volunteer Possibilities

Annual membership in the National Parks and Conservation Association is $25. There are special rates for libraries and students. Life memberships are $1,000. Members receive a one-year subscription to *National Parks*, published bimonthly.

NPCA has several volunteer opportunities. The park-watcher network consists of citizens across the United States who alert NPCA to park threats. There are now approximately 210 parks under the park-watch program, and a bimonthly newsletter, *Exchange,* keeps volunteers up-to-date and provides assistance.

NPCA also uses volunteers in its Washington, D.C. office. Volunteers at the home office assist the development department in tasks involving public relations, fund-raising, and coordinating events and trips.

NPCA's federal activities department offers internships to college students and graduates. These six- to eight-week internships involve work with the legislative process.

☐ NATIONAL TOXICS CAMPAIGN

1168 Commonwealth Avenue
Boston, MA 02134
(617) 232-0327
Contact: John O'Connor, Executive Director

History/Goals
The National Toxics Campaign is a network of 100,000 individual members and approximately 1,300 community and activist groups throughout the United States. NTC was founded in 1984 and has regional offices in Alabama, Maine, Oklahoma, North Carolina, Massachusetts, Colorado, California (three), Texas (two), and Louisiana.

NTC works at the grassroots level to prevent and solve this country's toxic and environmental problems.

Past Achievements
NTC forced Conoco to pay $23 million to 400 families in Ponca City, Oklahoma, who were forced from their homes by toxic wastes from the Conoco refinery.

Since 1984 NTC's western office in Denver, Colorado, has assisted the residents of the Friendly Hills subdivision just outside Denver in their fight against Martin Marietta and the Denver Water Board. Residents in the subdivision began organizing to investigate the deaths, cancers, birth defects, and diseases occurring in large numbers in the community. After discovering that Martin Marietta had been polluting the water source since the late 1950s, NTC and the citizens' group filed charges against Martin Marietta and the Denver Water Board. In early 1990 the U.S. District Court ruled that there was substantial evidence of a conspiracy between the defense contractor and the water board to cover up evidence about the pollutants, thereby depriving the residents of their civil rights. The case still has to go to trial.

NTC's Texas affiliate, Texans United, worked with a group of approximately 200 Highlands, Texas, residents to bring suit against Exxon for the Liberty Waste dumpsite. After lengthy negotiations and numerous studies conducted by both sides, Exxon agreed to an $11 million settlement in 1990. The site is now being investigated and will be considered for federal Superfund status.

NTC has developed a Grassroots Environmental Evaluation of Federal Facilities (GREEFF) Report Card. This report card rates military bases for their performance on base cleanup, toxic use, and their record on informing the public of issues. This report card is also part of a Military Toxics Starter Kit that has been produced to help citizens living near military bases organize and demand changes.

Ongoing Projects
NTC recently joined a new coalition, the Biotech Working Group, which is composed of eighteen environmental, farm, consumer, and church

organizations. The working group will study the use of biotechnology to make agricultural crops and forest trees genetically tolerant of chemical herbicides.

NTC works to get companies to sign "good neighbor" policies agreeing not to poison the environment. If the companies are found to be violating the agreement, NTC gathers evidence and takes the case to court.

NTC works with other environmental groups on projects concerning toxic wastes. NTC uses lobbyists, grassroots organizers, and media campaigns to put forward its positions. NTC produces a large number of publications continually. Some of the publications now available through NTC include *Fighting Toxics: A Manual for Protecting Your Family, Community, and Workplace*; *A Practical Strategy to Reduce Dangerous Pesticides in Our Food and the Environment*; *A Consumer's Guide to Protecting Your Drinking Water*; *Organizing to Win*; *Corporate Campaigns*; *Using the Media*; and *Researching and Obtaining Information*.

NTC operates the Citizens' Environmental Laboratory. This laboratory provides a low-cost, reliable testing method for communities believed to be at risk from toxic contamination. The lab is able to analyze water, soil, air, and waste samples and can quantify up to 56,000 different pesticides. The lab is open to any organizations that join the National Toxics Campaign.

Future Plans

NTC plans to push for policies that will allocate more money for environmental restoration and will pay reparations to communities devastated by toxic disasters. NTC hopes to help initiate policies requiring the military to reduce its use of toxic chemicals and the resultant wastes.

NTC will be publishing a comprehensive report on the environmental problems of military bases across the country.

Through the Biotech Working Group, NTC hopes to end research support for herbicide-tolerant plants; to stop the 20 percent federal tax credit given to private companies involved in herbicide tolerance research on crops and trees; to require the EPA to regulate herbicide-tolerant plants under the pesticide laws; to remove federal tax incentives that favor high-chemical agriculture; and to make it a law that Third World countries be informed of the potential hazards of herbicide-tolerant plants and trees.

Membership Information and Volunteer Possibilities

Annual membership in the National Toxics campaign is $15. Members receive a subscription to the quarterly magazine, *Toxic Times*.

Volunteer opportunities are available through the local offices, chapters, and affiliates. Local chapters organize grassroots support for NTC's campaigns, and members are encouraged to take an active role in the organization.

☐ NATIONAL WILDFLOWER RESEARCH CENTER
2600 FM 973
Austin, TX 78725
(512) 929-3600
Contacts: Dr. David K. Northington, Executive Director
Annie Paulson, Clearinghouse Coordinator
Mae Daniller, Director of Membership Services

History/Goals
The National Wildflower Research Center was founded in 1982 by Lady Bird Johnson as a research institute. The center works to promote the conservation, propagation, and use of wildflowers and natural grasses and trees in landscapes nationwide (both wild and planned).

The information gained through the center's extensive research is shared with the general public through education, publications, a national clearinghouse, and a strong membership located across the country.

Past Achievements
Since its founding in 1982, the center has been expanding its research facilities and public outreach programs.

A germinator, necessary for the germination of seed requiring a stable and constant temperature, was acquired.

An herbarium of pressed plants was established showing the seedling, mid-growth, and flowering stages of over 150 species.

A seed herbarium was begun. This herbarium contains catalogued field-collected seeds from over forty wildflower species.

The seedling identification project was begun to identify seedlings and record their subsequent stages. Plants are grown and then photographed at each stage of growth. Fifty species are already complete, and an additional fifty species have been grown and are in the process of being photographed.

Ongoing Projects
The center has research projects ongoing at all times and various greenhouses, shade houses, and other facilities have been built to accommodate this research.

Another major area where the center is active is in education and information gathering. The wildflower center offers teacher education programs, educational displays, seminars, training sessions, and demonstration plantings.

The National Wildflower Research Center contains the most comprehensive collection of wildflower information in the country. The clearinghouse answered a total of 35,200 inquiries between 1985 and 1987. A complete data base contains information on native plant nurseries, seed sources, and other organizations. A slide library holds 7,000 catalogued slides and is used for education and general presentations. The reference library contains 400 books, including manuals and field guides. More than 250 fact sheets are available to answer requests for specific information.

Future Plans

Researchers at the center plan to study wildflower mixes in different regions across the country and the use of wildflowers for erosion control. Research on large-scale wildflower planting in parks and along highways is a major priority for the future.

Several publications are being planned to bring more information to the public, including a wildflower source book, a full-color seedling identification book, and a resource book of educational activities and information designed for primary and secondary school teachers.

The center plans to develop a ten-minute video on wildflowers to be used in the classroom. There are plans to establish a national network of speakers, and to enlarge the libraries and the clearinghouse.

Membership Information and Volunteer Possibilities

Membership in the National Wildflower Research Center has grown dramatically in recent years. There are currently over 7,000 members, of which 45 percent are national members. Membership is $25 annually, and members receive a subscription to *Wildflower*, the newsletter and *Wildflower, Journal of the National Wildflower Research Center*, published semiannually. Members also have access to free information from the clearinghouse, advance notice of seminars, and discounts on items in the gift catalogue.

The center depends heavily on volunteers. Locally in Austin, volunteers have been recruited through the Retired Senior Volunteer Program. A newsletter is designed specifically for volunteers. Currently 110 volunteers serve the center.

Plans are being made to expand volunteer involvement across the country using the large national membership network. The establishment of a speakers' bureau will provide opportunities for volunteers across the country.

☐ NATIONAL WILDLIFE FEDERATION

1400 Sixteenth Street, NW
Washington, DC 20036–2266
(202) 797-6800
Contacts: Jay D. Hair, President
Catherine T. Malinin, Membership Action
Coordinator

History/Goals

In 1936 President Franklin D. Roosevelt convened the first North American Wildlife Conference in Washington, D.C. The purpose of the conference was to create an organization which would "make effective progress in restoring and conserving the vanishing wildlife resources of a continent." The General Wildlife Federation was that organization, and it was headed by Jay "Ding" Darling, a political cartoonist and Director of the U.S. Biological Survey. In 1938 its name was changed to the National Wildlife Federation. Today the federation is the largest environmental organization in the country, with over 5.6 million members and 52 affiliates throughout the country. Its primary objective continues to be the promotion of the wise use of our natural resources. This is accomplished through education programs, publications, and research activities. The federation cooperates with legislators, government agencies, and private groups, including other environmental organizations, to meet these goals.

The current president is Jay D. Hair, former administrator of the fisheries and wildlife sciences program at North Carolina State University.

Past Achievements

The federation helped develop a series of international environmental education programs with the Agency for International Development entitled "Our Threatened Heritage."

The federation has helped establish the Atchafalaya National Wildlife Refuge in Louisiana and the National Biotechnology Policy Center, which focuses on the environmental implications of biotechnology.

NWF won a lawsuit that stopped coal leasing in the Fort Union region of North Dakota until the federal coal program could be reformed. Another lawsuit required the Interior Department and the EPA to issue the necessary regulations required to implement the natural resource damage provision of Superfund.

NWF has established the Mountain Laurel Trail located at the Laurel Ridge Conservation Education Center in Vienna, Virginia. The trail, accessible to the physically challenged, features special paving, large-print interpretive signs, braille transcriptions of trail guides, and audiocassette–guided tours.

Ongoing Projects

Each year NWF sponsors National Wildlife Week. During the week, education kits and posters are sent to educators across the country. The week also features public service announcements to take the environmental message to the American public.

NWF has several successful educational programs. The federation publishes *Ranger Rick* magazine for children six to twelve years and *Your*

Big Backyard for preschoolers. These magazines focus on conservation issues for children.

NWF also has a science and social studies curriculum for middle schools, the CLASS Project. Education programs are also offered at the Laurel Ridge Conservation Education Center. NWF publishes NA-TURE-SCOPE, a science and nature activity series used to supplement the curriculum in the schools. NWF also sponsors a teen adventure program at NWF's wildlife camps in Colorado and North Carolina for youth ages fourteen to seventeen.

At the center in Virginia, NWF has a 10,000-volume conservation library useful for reference and research.

The federation produces a biweekly column featured in over 7,000 publications across the country entitled "The Backyard Naturalist."

The federation features four types of programs called annual summits. NWF's Wildlife Camps are open to children ages nine through thirteen, with Teen Adventures for fourteen- to seventeen-year-olds. NatureQuest is an environmental education program for camp and youth leaders; federation gives the three-day workshop at locations throughout the United States. Conservation Summits are designed for children and adults. These family-oriented summits are set at various locations throughout the country each year. The newest summits are designed to help teachers incorporate environmental education into the classroom. The first of these was held in 1989 in Estes Park, Colorado, and was attended by nearly 330 adults.

NWF operates seven resource conservation centers across the country, in Atlanta, Georgia; Ann Arbor, Michigan; Boulder, Colorado; Missoula, Montana; Bismarck, North Dakota; Portland, Oregon; and Anchorage, Alaska. These centers conduct investigations and pursue litigation and legislative campaigns.

The federation has numerous regional offices and affiliates throughout the United States. The oldest regional office is the Rocky Mountain Natural Resources Center, in Boulder, Colorado. This office works on projects such as water resources development and protection of federal lands. The office led the fight against the proposed Two Forks Dam project, which was struck down in late 1990. The newest regional office is the Alaska Natural Resources Center in Anchorage. This office deals with oil and gas exploration and development in remote and sensitive Arctic ecosystems. The center was busy following the Exxon Valdez oil spill. The center lobbied successfully in Alaska's state legislature for passage of bills to increase liability for companies that spill hazardous substances. Other regional offices—Great Lakes Natural Resources Center in Ann Arbor, Michigan; Northern Rockies Natural Resources Center in Missoula, Montana; the Pacific Northwest Natural Resources Center in Portland, Oregon; the Prairie Wetlands Natural Resources Center in

Bismarck, North Dakota; and the Southeastern Natural Resources Center in Atlanta, Georgia—focus on issues such as water quality standards, federal oil and gas leasing practices, preservation of ancient forests, blocking the building of a new dam, wetlands preservation, and the protection of fish and wildlife resources.

Future Plans
The National Wildlife Federation will continue its many programs into the future, including its educational programs, National Wildlife Week, and its educational publishing. The federation is planning on implementing on-line data bases accessible to natural resource professionals.

Membership Information and Volunteer Possibilities
Annual membership in the National Wildlife Federation is $15. Members receive a subscription to either *National Wildlife* or *International Wildlife*; for an extra fee, members can receive both. Children who join receive *Ranger Rick* as junior members. Members can receive discounts on selected books and merchandise and can attend the annual meetings. Members are also eligible to attend the Conservation Summits and Wildlife Camp at a special rate.

Volunteer opportunities exist in many areas of the National Wildlife Federation. Volunteers are used at the local level through the NWF affiliates. Members can join the Resource Conservation Alliance, which is a grassroots network of federation members. Alliance members receive action alerts and a newsletter to keep them up-to-date on current activities.

☐ NATURAL RESOURCES DEFENSE COUNCIL
40 West Twentieth Street
New York, NY 10011
(212) 727-2700
Contacts: John Adams, Executive Director
Marie Weinmann, Associate Director,
Membership

History/Goals
The Natural Resources Defense Council was founded in 1970 by a group of Yale Law School classmates. The council litigates cases and lobbies on causes such as energy policy, air and water pollution, and global warming. The executive director is John Adams, the first and only executive director of NRDC. Mr. Adams, a former U.S. attorney, was one of the original founders of the organization. Today there are over 168,000 members, making NRDC the country's ninth largest environmental organization. Besides the home office in New York, there are offices in Washington, D.C., San Francisco, Los Angeles, and Honolulu.

The NRDC works for the environment through litigation, advocacy, and research. NRDC's informational brochure sums up the organization's goals in a four-line quote: "The power of law. The power of science. The power of people. In defense of the environment."

Past Achievements

One of NRDC's most widely publicized campaigns was the 1989 battle against the chemical Alar, found on apples. With the aid of spokesperson Meryl Streep and the "Mothers and Others for Pesticide Limits" campaign, NRDC led the country's efforts to keep apples free of the chemical.

NRDC has won many lawsuits over the twenty years since its founding, such as: forcing polluters to stop illegal dumping in rivers, lakes, and streams; fighting federal coal-leasing and oil-drilling policies; the fight against acid rain; and work on the enforcement of the Clean Air Act.

In California and then at the national level, NRDC succeeded in getting new energy efficiency standards.

Ongoing Projects

NRDC is working to preserve the coastal environments in the United States, from New England to Alaska's Arctic National Wildlife Refuge. In late 1990 NRDC filed a lawsuit to protect the Arctic National Wildlife Refuge from new oil development.

NRDC has recently begun several projects with the Soviet Academy of Sciences. This relationship focuses on two major topics: nuclear weapons proliferation and global warming. NRDC initiated an exchange with the Academy of Sciences in which scientists from both countries monitor the superpower nuclear test ban. Other projects have included demonstration projects showing how carbon dioxide emissions can be reduced.

NRDC has begun a "Rescue the Rainforest" campaign, an effort to stop rain forest deforestation through the purchase of rain forest-inspired products. The products include T-shirts, books, and tapes.

Future Plans

The Natural Resources Defense Council plans to focus much future attention on the rain forests and plans to mobilize national public support for rain forest preservation. A new book, *The Rainforest Book*, will be distributed nationwide. NRDC hopes to pressure the U.S. Fish and Wildlife Service to implement the Endangered Species Act more efficiently and at a quicker pace to help stop deforestation in the United States. NRDC will also focus on reforming international lending policies and will attempt to pressure lending agencies to consider environmental consequences of their lending policies. Within the United States NRDC plans to expand land acquisition programs to include U.S. rain forests, and will pressure American corporations to reform investment, export, and import policies to take the rain forests into consideration.

Membership Information and Volunteer Possibilities
Annual membership in the Natural Resources Defense Council is a minimum of $10. Members receive NRDC's quarterly magazine, *The Amicus Journal*, and the *NRDC Newsline*, a newsletter published five times each year with updates on programs, publications, events, and news. Members also receive action alerts and NRDC updates, along with occasional postcard mailings to be sent to policy makers at the state and local levels in support of certain issues.

Members can participate in NRDC through the postcard mailings and by writing letters to legislatures and other government officials. There are also legal internships available as well as general internships for graduate and undergraduate students.

☐ THE NATURE CONSERVANCY
1815 North Lynn Street
Arlington, VA 22209
(703) 841-5394
Contact: John C. Sawhill, President

History/Goals
The Nature Conservancy was founded in 1951 to "find, protect, and maintain the Earth's rare species and natural communities by preserving the lands they need to survive." Today there are nearly 600,000 members in the conservancy, making it the country's fourth largest environmental organization. The conservancy manages nearly 1,100 preserves and holds land valued at nearly $400 million. The conservancy claims responsibility for the protection of 5.5 million acres of land in fifty states and Canada. It has also helped to preserve millions of acres in Latin America and the Caribbean. The conservancy has an annual budget of over $156 million, making it the country's richest environmental organization.

The Conservancy's primary objective is to locate key areas of land that need protection, to acquire the land, and to protect and maintain the land.

Past Achievements
During 1989 TNC completed 578 projects and safeguarded an additional 546,818 acres of land in the United States.

A working partnership was formed with the Bureau of Land Management in 1989 to protect 22,677 acres of land and 13,650 acre-feet of water in New Mexico, Nevada, California, and Oregon.

Through negotiations with government agencies, nearly 120,000 acres of forest and wetlands in four New England states were protected, including 15,391 acres and a conservation easement on nearly 40,000 additional acres for New York's Adirondack Park.

Over $9 million in debt-for-nature swaps during 1989 involved land in the Ecuadorian Andes, the Amazon, the Galapagos Islands, and Costa Rica.

An additional purchase of 7,637 acres in California's Carrizo Plain brought the total secured acreage to 89,523. This tract of land is host to more species of rare and endangered vertebrates than any other site in California. The land will be jointly managed by TNC and the BLM.

Ongoing Projects

The Nature Conservancy continues to acquire land for preservation. In a unique partnership with Ducks Unlimited, the conservancy is restoring the riparian forests and DU is restoring the wetlands in parts of Louisiana, California, South Dakota, Illinois, and South Carolina.

A major project in Colorado is the Rivers of the Rockies campaign. This project is a $5 million campaign over three years beginning in 1990 to preserve thirty sites on twenty Colorado rivers and tributaries. A similar project is being undertaken in Arizona to protect that state's critical riparian sites. There are numerous other such projects in numerous states throughout the country.

Future Plans

The Nature Conservancy continues to purchase lands for protection or to use as "trade lands," which are traded to the government or sold to private interests. The Nature Conservancy works closely with the BLM, the Fish & Wildlife Service, the U.S. Forest Service, and various other environmental organizations in managing lands throughout the country.

Membership Information and Volunteer Possibilities

Annual membership in The Conservancy is $15, and members receive a subscription to the quarterly magazine, *Nature Conservancy*. Members are also eligible to attend various Conservancy trips sponsored throughout the year in various parts of the country.

There are four regional offices of the Conservancy and field offices in nearly every state in the country. Volunteer opportunities are available through these local field offices. Volunteers can help at the many preserves, and there are often opportunities at the local offices, assisting with mailings and member services.

☐ NEW ALCHEMY INSTITUTE

237 Hatchville Road
East Falmouth, MA 02536
(508) 564-6301
Contact: Ann Milliman, Public Information Director

History/Goals

The New Alchemy Institute was founded in 1969 as a research and education center. The institute, located on twelve acres on Cape Cod, Massachusetts, serves students, teachers, households, and small-scale farmers through information, research, demonstration projects, and education projects. The major areas of concentration at the institute are landscape design, organic market gardening, farmer outreach, integrated pest management, cover cropping, composting, and greenhouse horticulture.

Past Achievements

The New Alchemy Institute has set up a twelve-acre living laboratory. In 1976 the Cape Cod Ark was built. The Ark is a greenhouse, heated by the sun and home to pesticide-free food year-round. The Ark is complete with soil, food crops, beneficial insects, and aquaculture ponds to provide a balanced ecosystem.

The institute has also completed the New Alchemy House, a demonstration of a practical, affordable, energy-efficient house. The house demonstrates energy efficiency, water conservation, effective waste treatment, and year-round food production. A monitoring program has been established around the house.

Ongoing Projects

Each year the institute has thousands of visitors. A visitor's center and store provide exhibits, slide shows, books, tools, and garden supplies.

Research projects are ongoing at the institute. The institute is currently working with twenty New England farmers testing integrated pest management and cover cropping systems. The research is designed to develop methods to sustain soil fertility, control weeds, and reduce erosion without chemicals or herbicides. The research is conducted with the support of local farmers, who have input into the planning and the research process.

New Alchemy offers a sixteen-week Semester at New Alchemy for third-year college students. The on-site program includes courses in sustainable agriculture, community resource systems, ecological home technologies, and applied studies.

The institute has an extensive children's program. Classes in organic gardening and nature studies are available in the summer. Fall programs are designed for children and their parents, and a school program is available throughout the school year. The institute offers a training manual for teachers, and teacher workshops at schools or at the institute.

Events are ongoing throughout the year at the New Alchemy Institute. On-site workshops are offered, featuring guest speakers. A speakers series each spring brings lectures on ecology and community development. The annual summer open house encourages learning in a more informal setting. A "Fun Run in the Sun" each August is held to support children's programs. The annual fall harvest festival is the biggest event of the year, featuring keynote speakers, ideas, entertainment, food, and activities.

Future Plans

New Alchemy has a master plan that includes several picture programs. Among these are theme gardens, a new library and classroom, expansion of the market garden, and the addition of 5,000 square feet of greenhouses, energy-efficient and pesticide-free.

Membership Information and Volunteer Possibilities

Annual membership in New Alchemy Institute is $35. Reduced memberships of $20 are available to students and those on fixed incomes. Life memberships are available for $1,000. Members receive a subscription to *New Alchemy Quarterly*. The magazine is also available to nonmembers for $8 annually. Members also receive admission to guided tours at the institute, notification of all special events and courses, and get 20 percent off all courses, workshops, and any purchases at the visitors' center or from the new catalog.

There are many volunteer opportunities at the Institute. Volunteers help with the gardens, landscaping, meeting and greeting visitors, and doing mailings. There are also approximately twenty internships available annually. Interns work for at least twenty hours each week and stay at the institute for one to six months.

☐ NEW ENGLAND WILD FLOWER SOCIETY

Hemenway Road
Framingham, MA 01701
(617) 237-4024 or (508) 877-7630
Contact: David Longland, Executive Director

History/Goals

The New England Wild Flower Society was established in 1922 to promote the conservation of native plants. To meet its goal, the society conducts research and education in botany, horticulture, and ecology.

Past Achievements

The society has established a forty-five-acre botanic garden, Garden in the Woods, in Framingham, Massachusetts. Wooded paths take visitors past 1,500 varieties of native plants, including many rare and endangered species. The gardens are open to the general public from mid-April through October.

Ongoing Projects

The society sponsors education programs in which regional experts teach courses on plant identification, wildflower gardening, and natural history. Field trips are often made to private gardens and natural habitat areas.

The society publishes a wide range of publications, including *Nursery Source List* and *Wild Flower Notes*. The Lawrence Newcomb Library, from which members may borrow books, has an extensive slide library in addition to the wide-ranging botanical books.

Future Plans

The society plans to continue its current programs and research projects. New propagation techniques for common and rare species are being researched. Plants and seeds are available to the public in the hopes that people will grow and enjoy wildflowers at home.

Membership Information and Volunteer Possibilities

Individual membership in the New England Wild Flower Society is $30 annually. An annual family membership is available for $35. Members receive society publications; discounts on books, plants, and items from the gift shop; free admission to Garden in the Woods; and borrowing privileges at the Lawrence Newcomb Library.

There are active state chapters throughout New England with individual newsletters and special programs. There are also six sanctuaries in three New England states designed for the preservation of plants in their natural habitats.

☐ NORTH AMERICAN ASSOCIATION FOR ENVIRONMENTAL EDUCATION

P.O. Box 400
Troy, OH 45373
(513) 698-6493
Contact: Joan C. Heidelberg, Executive Vice President

History/Goals

The North American Association for Environmental Education was established nearly twenty years ago and today has over 1,000 members from all over the United States, Canada, Mexico, and a dozen other countries. NAAEE works to help bring environmental information to those who teach about the environment. Members include teachers, students, writers, naturalists, managers, and filmmakers. NAAEE serves as a network for the professionals in the field and as experts on policy, standards, and materials development. NAAEE hopes to help create a healthy environment by encouraging people to explore issues, raise important questions, investigate new ideas, and seek solutions to environmental problems.

Past Achievements

NAAEE has published many works in the two decades since its founding. One of its largest projects was the completion of a data base for activities and programs titled *Essential Learnings in Environmental Education*. This fully indexed publication is a listing of 600 concepts that should be included in any environmental education curriculum. The handbook is divided into three sections: Natural Systems, which includes weather and other physical systems, the biosphere, ecosystems, evolution, and extinction; Resources, including distribution, consumption, conservation, pollution, water, energy, and forests; and Human Systems, including sections on technology, agriculture, population, economics, religion and ethics, legislation, and individual action.

Ongoing Projects

NAAEE's programs are divided into four sections to enable the organization to better handle the diversity of its members: The elementary and secondary education section is involved in issues such as educational research, curriculum development, teacher training, and incorporating environmental education into the schools; the non-formal section focuses on those working outside the schools, such as those involved in environmental education at nature centers, museums, parks, zoos, and government agencies; the environmental studies section helps address the concerns of faculty and students at the college and university level; and the conservation education section is designed for those who develop educational programs focusing on conservation and natural resources.

NAAEE's annual conference is open to all members. This five-day conference gives members a chance to attend workshops, seminars, presentations, and other formal and informal activities.

NAAEE produces a variety of publications on an ongoing basis. Publications include conference proceedings, monographs, recent graduate works, resource catalogs, film and video catalogs, and workshop guides.

Future Plans

NAAEE hopes to provide greater services to its members, such as a comprehensive data base of environmental education materials, programs, and experts. There are also plans to expand the conference and publications programs. Over the long term, NAAEE hopes to have greater interaction with state, regional, and international organizations and plans to increase networking and information access via telecommunications networks.

Membership Information and Volunteer Possibilities

Annual membership in the North American Association for Environmental Education is $35. A reduced student membership is available for $20 and a life membership for $400. Members receive a subscription to the bimonthly newsmagazine, *Environmental Communicator*, along with complimentary copies of new NAAEE publications and discounts on additional publications. Members receive bonus time on EcoNet, the official electronic communication system of NAAEE, and subscription discounts on magazines such as *Journal of Environmental Education, Science Education, Environment*, and *The Environmentalist*.

Board members are volunteers, and some of the committees utilize volunteers.

☐ THE NORTH AMERICAN BLUEBIRD SOCIETY

Box 6295
Silver Springs, MD 20916–6295
(301) 384-2798
Contact: Mary D. Janetatos, Executive Director

History/Goals
The North American Bluebird Society was established in 1978 to alert the public to the decrease of the three species of North American bluebirds and to rebuild that population.

The society's goals are to study the obstacles impeding the recovery of the bluebird, such as severe weather and a lack of nesting sites; to promote ideas and actions to counter the obstacles, such as the building of nesting boxes and the establishment of trails; and to obtain more complete information on bluebirds and establish scientific records.

Past Achievements
The society has gathered together 5,500 members since its founding. It has been effective in promoting bluebird trails in which nesting boxes are placed at least 100 yards apart.

Ongoing Projects
The society conducts ongoing research to determine factors such as effective nesting box design, control of competitors and predators, and enhanced techniques for increasing winter food supply.

The society provides information to the public through lectures and demonstrations to schools, slide shows, media campaigns, and a speakers' bureau.

Future Plans
The society will continue to promote the survival of the North American Bluebird through increased public awareness and research programs.

Membership Information and Volunteer Possibilities
Annual membership in The North American Bluebird Society is $15, and there are reduced-price memberships for students and seniors; a life membership is available for $500.

Members receive a subscription to the quarterly journal, *SIALIA,* as well as the chance to purchase society literature, art, and gifts at discounted prices.

The society depends on members at the local level. Members are encouraged to build nesting boxes, organize bluebird trails, and report observational data to the society.

☐ NORTH AMERICAN LOON FUND

R.R. 4, Box 240C
Meredith, NH 03253
(603) 279-6163
Contacts: Linda O'Bara, Director
Julie Grablewski, Office Manager

History/Goals

The North American Loon Fund was founded in 1979 to help preserve loons and their habitats in the United States. The fund conducts research, offers public education, and publishes scientific reports.

The organization consists of scientists, educators, businesspeople, and private individuals. There are fourteen affiliated organizations across the United States and Canada, and there are currently 2,000 members.

Past Achievements

Since 1981 NALF has sponsored over 125 research projects and has given over $200,000 in support of these projects. NALF has successfully documented the effects of lake acidification on loons and has established a way to use the yodel vocalizations of the male loons for positive individual identifications.

Since its founding NALF has sponsored a number of scientific conferences that focus on loon research and management.

A production company has worked with NALF to put together an educational package for kindergarten through adult audiences. The package, "Loons and Life," includes twelve lesson plans, the videotape *Loons,* NALF's audiocassette "Voices of the Loon," and a poster.

Ongoing Projects

NALF is working in western Massachusetts to protect a new breeding population of loons in that area. In Montana the fund is working to establish a management plan for the loons.

NALF continually awards research grants as well as grants for educational programs and management programs. The fund sells a variety of loon merchandise to support these programs. NALF also publishes scientific and other documents on an ongoing basis. NALF also has created a file of technical documents, which it routinely makes available to the public and the scientific community.

NALF has been working with Exxon Company USA, which is funding yellow-billed loon research in Alaska. Through this research grant, NALF researchers conduct aerial and ground surveys on Alaska's North Slope.

Future Plans

NALF is planning a comprehensive bibliography of scientific papers on loons. The organization will continue to pursue its objectives of protecting the loon populations in the United States and studying the loons and their habitat.

Membership Information and Volunteer Possibilities
Annual membership in the North American Loon Fund is $25. Family memberships are $35. Members receive the quarterly newsletter, *The Loon Call*, as well as listings of merchandise and an invitation to attend the annual meetings.

Volunteer activities are organized through the various affiliates across the United States Volunteers can work to help protect lake habitats and the loons themselves. Volunteers participate in monitoring the populations, and in educating the public about the needs of loons.

☐ NORTH AMERICAN WILDLIFE FOUNDATION

102 Wilmot Road, Suite 410
Deerfield, IL 60015
(708) 940-7776
Contacts: Bonnie Zambos, Office Assistant
Charles S. Potter, Jr., Executive Vice President

History/Goals
The North American Wildlife Foundation was created in 1911 to address the environmental issues of soil and water conservation, wetlands management, and wildlife preservation through research, education, and communications. Today there are over 8,000 members in the United States and Canada.

Past Achievements
The foundation has established the Delta Research Station (see below) and has completed numerous research projects. Delta was the first research facility to breed both the trumpeter swan and canvasback in captivity. In the 1950s Delta refined a sex and age determination technique that is now commonly used in breeding surveys and harvest analyses worldwide.

Ongoing Projects
The principal project of the foundation is the Delta Waterfowl and Wetlands Research Station, located on the 50,000-acre Delta Marsh in Manitoba, Canada. The Delta Research Station is home to a variety of research projects undertaken by graduate students.

The foundation has developed the NAWF Voluntary Restrain Program. This program was developed by sportsmen to ensure the continued quality of wildfowl.

NAWF also periodically produces movies and videos on waterfowl issues, along with handbooks on marsh management, breeding grounds habitat management, and wintering grounds management.

Future Plans
The Delta Research Station will continue to be one of NAWF's major projects. The station will continue to train researchers and to provide

information to organizations, individuals, and government agencies. The foundation plans to expand some of the research and education programs at the station to better address critical issues such as wetlands preservation on the prairies of the United States and Canada.

One of NAWF's newest programs is the prairie farming program. Through this innovative program the foundation plans to bring together agriculture and waterfowl experts to research and then implement land-use practices on the North American prairies.

NAWF also plans to broaden its communications program, allowing for more information to reach the general public about the plight of waterfowl and wetlands and to promote programs in sustainable agriculture.

Membership Information and Volunteer Possibilities
There is no actual membership fee, but a minimum donation of $20 is requested. Members receive the quarterly *Waterfowl Report* and the *Annual State of Prairie Ducks Report.*

The innovative prairie farming program is a grassroots program. Farmers and other agricultural experts are encouraged to assist voluntarily in this program, aimed at bringing about long-term land-use changes to promote farm profitability, environmental quality, and preservation of waterfowl populations.

☐ OCEAN ALLIANCE
Building E, Fort Mason Center
San Francisco, CA 94123
(415) 441-5970
Contacts: Margaret Elliott, Executive Officer

History/Goals
Ocean Alliance was formed to protect our water resources and the plant and animal life in them. The alliance hopes to accomplish this goal by fighting pollution and other abuses and by promoting conservation, education, and research.

Ocean Alliance was established in 1978. In 1990 the alliance was reorganized when it merged with the Whale Center (established in 1978) and the San Francisco Bay Chapter of Oceanic Society. The alliance currently has 3,000 members.

Past Achievements
Ocean Alliance has helped to establish National Marine Sanctuaries in California at Gulf of the Farallones, Cordell Bank, and the Channel Islands.

A long-term campaign to save dolphins from tuna fleets paid off in 1990. The National Marine Fisheries Service placed a ban on the use of explosives by tuna fishermen in herding dolphins. The ban applies only to U.S. boats, but tuna from those countries using explosives is also banned from importation into the United States. Major tuna companies also announced a ban on all tuna from fishermen who harm dolphins in any way.

Ongoing Projects

Ocean Alliance supports a variety of conservation and education programs. Project Ocean is a science curriculum for schools that brings the ocean to the kids. Whale Bus is a traveling classroom that brings hands-on learning with slides and songs to schools, community centers, and libraries. The Adopt-a-Whale program "adopts" whales and uses the donors' proceeds to help protect whales from commercial whalers. Sea Camp, for children ages six to fourteen, offers hands-on experience with tide-pools, beaches, and museums. The Adopt-a-Beach program recruits groups to care for a patch of beach. Sailing Education Adventures (SEA), a program designed for adults, teaches sailing. Sail Camp is designed to bring the world of sailing to those between eleven and fifteen years of age. Farallon Patrol serves as a lifeline and mode of transportation for volunteers at the Point Reyes Bird Observatory on the Farallon Islands.

Future Plans

One of Ocean Alliance's major goals is to integrate modern conservation concepts with marine science education programs and to increase the efforts to educate the general public.

The alliance is also working to ensure that California's Monterey Bay be designated a National Maritime Sanctuary.

Membership Information and Volunteer Possibilities

Membership in Ocean Alliance is $30 annually for an individual, $35 for families, and $20 for seniors/students. Membership is open to "any person dedicated to the preservation of our oceans and the San Francisco ecosystem for present and future generations." Members receive the alliance's publication, *Ocean Ally*, its periodic conservation updates, and discounts on programs and events.

Participation in the organization is primarily through the conservation and education programs in the San Francisco Bay Area.

☐ PACIFIC WHALE FOUNDATION

Kealia Beach Plaza
101 N. Kihei Road, Suite 21
Kihei, Maui, HI 96753–2615
(808) 879-8860
Contacts: Gregory D. Kaufman, President
Susan J. Eads, Program Administrator

History/Goals

The Pacific Whale Foundation was established in 1980 to conduct scientific research and educational programs, and to promote public awareness of whales, dolphins, and porpoises. The organization's 5,000 members include conservationists, scientists, and volunteers. PWF's major goal is to identify and study the factors adverse to the recovery of endangered marine mammals and to initiate actions against those factors.

Past Achievements

Since 1980 Pacific Whale Foundation has been involved in humpback whale research and in various marine conservation/education programs.

PWF has made initial contact with a large number of marine mammals and continues to track those animals.

Ongoing Projects

Pacific Whale Foundation claims to "bring learning to life" through various educational programs, including lectures to schools and community groups, whale-watch trips, brochures, and action alerts. The organization maintains a speakers' bureau and a library on marine mammals, and compiles statistics.

One of PWF's biggest programs is its Adopt-a-Whale Program. For an "adoption fee," concerned citizens can adopt a whale and will receive updates on sightings of the whale. Members who adopt a whale also receive a subscription to the biannual newsletter, *Soundings*.

PWF has two oceangoing vessels that are utilized in the educational programs. Whale One and Whale II are used for whale-watching, natural history cruises, and snorkeling trips.

Future Plans

Pacific Whale Foundation continues its efforts to conduct and support marine mammal research. PWF is currently studying the effects of increased human activity in the breeding grounds of the humpback whale in Hawaii. The results of the study will be analyzed and recommendations made based on the findings.

Membership Information and Volunteer Possibilities

Annual membership in Pacific Whale Foundation is $20 for an individual, $25 for a family. There are reduced memberships available for students and senior citizens. Members receive a subscription to the quarterly journal, *Fin & Fluke Report*, periodic action alerts, and discounts on merchandise, cruises, expeditions, and internship programs. Members may also use the foundation's library. Those who choose to adopt a whale also receive a subscription to *Soundings*, published two times each year. Interns receive *Whale One Dispatch*, the periodic internship newsletter.

☐ THE PEREGRINE FUND

5666 W. Flying Hawk Lane
Boise, ID 83709
(208) 362-3716
Contact: William A. Burnham, President and Director

History/Goals
The Peregrine Fund was created in 1970 at Cornell University by Dr. Tom Cade. Dr. Cade's goal was to prevent the expected extinction of the peregrine by releasing captive-produced young. The Peregrine Fund has been doing just that since then and projects a complete recovery of peregrine falcons in the United States by the year 2000.

Today's goal for the Peregrine Fund is the "conservation of birds of prey of the world and the environments they require." The current chairman of the Board of the Peregrine Fund is Roy E. Disney.

Past Achievements
Originally the fund worked out of three regional field offices in New York, Colorado, and California (Santa Cruz Predatory Bird Research Group). A permanent facility and headquarters, the World Center for Birds of Prey, was built in 1984 in Boise, Idaho, which consolidated the New York and Colorado offices.

Over the past twenty years, 3,800 raptors of twenty-two species of eagles, hawks, falcons, and owls have been raised. Over 3,000 peregrines have been released to the wild in twenty-eight states.

Researchers from the fund have cooperated on projects in thirty-five countries involving over fifty species of raptors.

The Peregrine Fund established and continues to cooperate in a graduate degree program in raptor biology at Boise State University in Idaho.

Ongoing Projects
The education program at the World Center for Birds of Prey aims at increasing public awareness and understanding of birds of prey. Through center tours, school and community programs, and information booths, the Peregrine Fund reaches thousands of people annually. The Archives of American Falconry is also located in the World Center. This collection of books, photographs, correspondence, and unique items serves as another way to reach the public.

The research facilities at the center allow researchers to study the behavior and reproductive biology of captured birds. Biologists can study and observe up to sixty pairs of falcons at the center.

Programs have been initiated in Guatemala, Iceland, Madagascar, and the Philippines, along with other countries around the world, to study species, reintroduce species, and preserve endangered forests. The Peregrine Fund also works closely with the Santa Cruz Predatory Bird Research Group at the University of California.

Future Plans

The techniques developed by The Peregrine Fund to help peregrines are being utilized by scientists all over the world in preserving numerous rare and endangered birds. The Peregrine Fund hopes that its research and techniques will contribute significantly to bird populations worldwide.

Membership Information and Volunteer Possibilities

Annual membership in The Peregrine Fund is $25. There are lower rates for students and seniors. Members are kept aware of the organization's progress through various mailings, newsletters, and an annual report. Volunteers can assist with ongoing projects in the organization. Tours are provided for visitors to the center.

☐ PROGRAMME FOR BELIZE

P.O. Box 1088
Vineyard Haven, MA 02568
(202) 293-4800
Contact: World Wildlife Fund

History/Goals

The Programme for Belize was established in 1988 by a consortium of international organizations. The founding donor of PFB was the Massachusetts Audubon Society. The program was established when the government of Belize invited conservation organizations to participate in the country's efforts at linking development and conservation in satisfactory and efficient ways. Programme for Belize is endorsed by the Audubon Alliance; Belize Audubon Society; Belize Center for Environmental Studies; Belize Zoo and Tropical Education Center; Manomet Bird Observatory; Massachusetts Audubon Society; Missouri Botanical Garden; National Audubon Society; Nature Conservancy; New York Zoological Society; and World Wildlife Fund.

Past Achievements

The Programme for Belize received an operating agreement from the government of Belize that gives PFB the permission to acquire and hold property in trust for the local people of Belize.

During PFB's first eighteen months of existence, a Conservation Department was established in Belize. Also during that time, PFB purchased 110,000 acres of tropical forest. This established the beginnings of the Rio Bravo Conservation and Management Area in Belize. Coca-Cola Foods transferred to PFB an additional 42,000 acres of adjacent tropical forest. An additional 130,000 acres still held by the original owner of the 110,000-acre tract will be managed as part of the preserve, bringing the total holdings up to 282,000 acres of tropical forest. A research station has also been established at the preserve.

Ongoing Projects

The program carries out research projects that seek to understand the biodiversity of the preserve and also looks at ways to utilize the resources of the area without destroying the environment in the preserve.

A professional training project has been established to help train Belizeans in conservation-related fields.

PFB is working to encourage a program sponsored by National Geographic. This program, known as "La Ruta Maya," is an attempt to encourage tourism in the area and to illustrate the rich Mayan history there.

Future Plans

Programme for Belize will continue to work with the government of Belize to preserve the land in that country and to train the local citizens in techniques necessary to develop and preserve the environment.

Membership Information and Volunteer Possibilities

There is no formal membership in the Programme for Belize; however, those who contribute to it receive a certificate of appreciation. A $50 donation is necessary to "purchase" and protect an acre of the Belizean tropical forest.

Groups and individuals across the United States have undertaken fundraising projects on behalf of the program. Supporters have formed U.S. networks that cooperate to promote the ideals of PFB and to raise money to support its programs.

☐ QUAIL UNLIMITED

P.O. Box 10041
Augusta, GA 30903
(803) 637-5731
Contact: Joseph R. Evans, Executive Vice President

History/Goals

Quail Unlimited was founded in 1981 and is dedicated to the preservation of quail and upland birds through habitat conservation. There are currently 14 state groups and 250 local groups with a total of over 44,000 members. Quail Unlimited is primarily an organization of bird hunters.

Past Achievements

Since its founding QU has planted over a quarter of a million trees, the majority of them in the Great Plains region to improve winter habitat for upland game species.

Quail Unlimited has also established a data base and has a mailing list available to other organizations.

Ongoing Projects

Quail Unlimited is involved in several programs: food and cover plantings; Project YIELD (Youth Involvement in Educational Land Development); prescribed burnings to manage land; public education; and the purchase of specialized equipment.

The QU seed program sees that grain seed is distributed to landowners for planting food strips around fields and food plots.

The organization has spent close to $100,000 to purchase equipment such as drip torches, root plows, tree and shrub planters, and other equipment necessary for farmers, land managers, or hunting clubs.

Some of the local QU chapters support programs to cover the cost of planting or to pay incentives to those landowners who encourage habitat improvement on their land. QU claims that as a direct benefit of this program, landowners will be more likely to allow hunting on their land and that the improved habitat will provide for a higher carrying capacity for the quail and other game birds. To date, QU has planted a total of over 100,000 square miles of food and cover plots.

Project YIELD is aimed at educating the bird hunters of tomorrow. The program sponsors youth seminars to give the children hands-on experience in planting food plots. The seminars are also used to teach safe, ethical hunting and gun-handling techniques. The project works with other organizations such as Future Farmers of America and 4-H Clubs.

The local QU chapters raise funds for statewide projects. Of all the monies collected by the local chapters, 60 percent goes for specific local projects, 20 percent goes to state wildlife agencies, 10 percent goes to develop additional chapters, and the remaining 10 percent goes to national projects of Quail Unlimited.

Future Plans

Quail Unlimited will continue to work toward the goal of habitat preservation. It will continue to sponsor research projects and to work with children in Project YIELD.

Membership Information and Volunteer Possibilities

Annual membership in Quail Unlimited is $30. Members receive a subscription to *Quail Unlimited* magazine, published bimonthly. For an annual fee of $50, members also can receive a QU conservation stamp, a certificate, and discounts on limited-edition wildlife art. Sponsor membership is available for $200 annually and entitles members to the magazine subscription, the benefits of charter membership, plus a signed and numbered annual stamp print, and a hat, lapel pin, and decal.

Volunteer activities are done through the local groups. Members are also encouraged to start chapters in their own local area if none has been previously established.

☐ RACHEL CARSON COUNCIL

8940 Jones Mill Road
Chevy Chase, MD 20815
(301) 652-1877
Contacts: Shirley A. Briggs, Executive Director
Dr. Samuel S. Epstein, President

History/Goals
The Rachel Carson Council was established in 1965 as the Rachel Carson
Trust for the Living Environment. The organization was founded at the
wish of Rachel Carson to further her causes and philosophies in the fight
against chemical contamination. The council's major focus remains on
chemical contamination, in particular the pesticide issues addressed in
Ms. Carson's book, *Silent Spring*. To this end the council works to
educate the public and promote an interest in the environment; encourages conservation measures; and also serves as a clearinghouse of information for the general public and the scientific community.

Past Achievements
Since its founding the Rachel Carson Council has done research on the
problem of chemical contamination. The council has also published a
large number of books and research information.

Ongoing Projects
The council continues to publish a number of books and pamphlets. The
library of books, periodicals, and files is constantly reviewed by scientists, environmentalists, and the general public.

Since the 1972 Stockholm conference, the Council has played a major
role in developing materials and making suggestions for the United
Nations Environment Program and specifically for the U.S. delegation.

The council has recently begun a cooperative program with the
National Coalition Against the Misuse of Pesticides. This cooperative
effort will combine the resources of both organizations. Questions about
specific pesticides will be handled by NCAMP.

Future Plans
One of the council's major goals for the future is the completion of a
basic guide to pesticides. This guide will represent a summation of
twenty-five years of study and experience and will include an analysis of
over 600 major pesticide ingredients. This project is expected to require
additional funds and personnel over several years.

The council also has plans to expand its library and to make analysis,
interpretation, and publication easier through new programs. The council would like to make the most current information available to the
largest possible number of people.

Membership Information and Volunteer Possibilities
Annual membership in the Rachel Carson Council is $15 and includes a
one-year subscription to the newsletter. Members also receive all council
publications free for the year of membership.

Members can participate in the council through monetary contributions, bequests, and deferred giving and by passing along the message of the council. There are no other formal volunteer possibilities available.

☐ RAILS-TO-TRAILS CONSERVANCY

1400 Sixteenth Street, NW
Washington, DC 20036
(202) 797-5400
Contacts: David G. Burwell, President
Maria Rothman, Membership Manager

History/Goals
Rail-to-Trails Conservancy was founded in 1985 by trails enthusiasts. RTC offers technical assistance, public education, advocacy, and negotiation, and pursues the legislation and regulatory action necessary to help establish trails on abandoned railroad right-of-ways across the United States. At the end of 1989 RTC had established over 242 trails, covering over 3,100 miles.

RTC currently has over 60,000 members throughout the country. There is a national office in Washington, D.C. and chapters in Illinois, Michigan, Ohio, Pennsylvania, and Washington State.

Past Achievements
During 1989 alone, RTC proposed over 3,000 miles of railroad right-of-way for trails. The land was to be abandoned and returned to the private sector before RTC intervened.

RTC has won several court cases that were brought by landowners who sought to prevent the development of trails along abandoned railroads.

RTC conducted a study during 1989 at the request of the National Park Service, which analyzed all abandoned rail corridors along the route of the North Country Trail. This proposed 3,200-mile trail, which is approximately 30 percent complete, will stretch from New York to North Dakota.

In early 1990 RTC released a historical study, *Railroads Recycled: How Local Initiative and Public Support Launched the Rails-to-Trails Movement, 1965–1990.* This report was the result of a joint study with the National Park Service.

RTC published *A Guide to America's Rail-Trails* and updated the publication during 1988 and 1989. The guide is RTC's most popular and covers nearly 200 existing rail-trails, providing a brief overview of the trails. RTC also published the more detailed *Sampler of America's Rail-Trails,* which gives an in-depth description of the trails along with color photographs, detailed maps, and surveys of public amenities in the surrounding areas.

Ongoing Projects

RTC works to secure the rest of the railways necessary to complete the 3200-mile North Country Trail.

RTC has an ongoing educational program designed to let the public know about the benefits of rail trails. During 1989 RTC sponsored a traveling seminar series entitled "Creating Trails from Abandoned Railroad Corridors." This series was attended by more than 215 public officials throughout the United States. The National Park Service helped fund the seminars and is doing so on a continuing basis. RTC has also published a slide show to present its goals and projects to the public; a videotape version is also available. RTC continues to publish other types of information on an ongoing basis.

RTC has developed a Visa card that is offered to members. RTC receives $10 for each new account opened and a percentage of every retail sale made with the card.

Future Plans

Rails-to-Trails Conservancy currently works in over thirty states to preserve abandoned rails as trails for public use. RTC plans to continue this work and to expand it wherever there are abandoned rails that can be converted.

Membership Information and Volunteer Possibilities

Annual membership in RTC is $18. Family memberships are $25. Members receive a subscription to RTC's quarterly newsletter, *Trailblazer*, along with discounts on a *Rails-to-Trails Citizen's Manual* and other publications. Members are also eligible to attend RTC-sponsored conferences and workshops at a discounted fee.

Volunteer opportunities are available through the local chapters, which provide technical assistance, public education, coalition building, and advocacy. These functions are made possible through volunteer networks.

☐ RAINFOREST ACTION NETWORK

301 Broadway, Suite A
San Francisco, CA 94133
(415) 398-4404
Contact: Randy Hayes, Director

History/Goals

Rainforest Action Network was founded in 1985 by Randy Hayes, formerly of Earth First! RAN works to protect tropical rain forests and the human rights of those living in the forests. The group works to bring the plight of the rain forests to the public's attention in countries where there are no tropical rain forests. There are currently 30,000 members in Rainforest Action Network.

Past Achievements
In RAN's first direct-action campaign, the group led a nationwide boycott of Burger King to protest the importation of cheap beef from countries where rain forests are clear-cut to make room for the cattle. During the 1987 boycott, Burger King's sales dropped 12 percent. The fast-food franchise responded by canceling $35 million worth of Central American beef contracts. The campaign was also successful in bringing the plight of the tropical forests to the attention of the American public.

Ongoing Projects
Rainforest Action Network established Rainforest Action Groups (RAGs) during the Burger King boycott. There are currently over 150 RAGs in the United States that carry out RAN's grassroots work and help organize local citizens to exert pressure on behalf of certain causes.

Consumer education is an ongoing effort of RAN. One of the major focuses of this part of RAN's work is the tropical timber trade. RAN has been calling for a ban on the importation and consumption of tropical timber and timber products.

RAN has established a network of over sixty environmental and human rights organizations worldwide. Through this network, RAN shares information and coordinates campaigns.

RAN has developed a slide show describing rain forest ecology, its destruction, and what can be done to help the rain forests.

Future Plans
Rainforest Action Network plans to continue its direct-action approach to the rain forest devastation. RAN will continue in its efforts to ban tropical timber imports. RAN has also recently begun a new campaign aimed at protecting the remaining lowland tropical rain forest in the United States.

Membership Information and Volunteer Possibilities
Annual membership in Rainforest Action Network is a minimum of $15. Members receive the quarterly news magazine, *World Rainforest Report*, along with monthly action alerts and any special mailings on rain forest issues.

RAN is a direct-action group that gets its support from the grassroots level. Members are urged to join one of 150 Rainforest Action Groups in the United States that work to educate local communities and gather support for boycotts or other direct-action campaigns. RAN encourages members to write letters to government officeholders and to participate in nonviolent public demonstrations. RAN also has a lengthy list of "Things to Do" for its members, including such actions as boycotting tropical wood products; sending letters to leaders of countries where tropical forests are being destroyed, such as Malaysia; writing to the President of the World Bank urging that institution to halt the funding of rain forest dams and to encourage the World Bank to fund small-scale projects that would benefit the inhabitants of the forests; writing to the Secretary General of the United Nations concerning development policies; boycotting all fast-food hamburgers or processed beef products; and requesting beef-labeling laws from the Secretary of Agriculture to identify the country of origin on all processed beef products.

☐ RAINFOREST ALLIANCE
270 Lafayette, Suite 512
New York, NY 10012
(212) 941-1900
Contact: Daniel R. Katz, Executive Director

History/Goals
The Rainforest Alliance was founded in 1986 and currently has over 2,500 members. The alliance links together professional organizations, financial institutions, scientists, the business community, conservationists, and citizens concerned with the conservation of the world's rain forests. The alliance supports education, research, active public involvement, and cooperation among organizations.

Past Achievements
The Rainforest Alliance opened a news bureau in San Jose, Costa Rica, in 1989. The Tropical Conservation News Bureau is designed to give the alliance access to firsthand information. The alliance also signed an agreement with Hermés of Paris to sell silk scarves with rainforest motifs for the alliance.

Ongoing Projects
Rainforest Alliance is a grassroots organization that prefers negotiations to boycotts. Rainforest Alliance favors regulation, rather than a ban, of tropical timber imports. The alliance administers The Kleinhans Fellowship, which researches sustainable uses of the rain forest without destroying it. The alliance also brought together experts under the Tropical Timber Project to develop guidelines to help consumers who purchase tropical timber products.

The alliance has strong educational and public information programs that include slide shows, a speaker series, fact sheets, a teacher's curriculum packet, conferences, newsletters, and consumer awareness brochures.

The alliance is currently raising money that will one day go to enlarge Costa Rica's Monteverde Cloud Forest Reserve. The alliance works regularly with Third World groups in protecting the rights of the people indigenous to the rain forests. The alliance is also an international clearinghouse of information.

Future Plans
The alliance is currently developing The Periwinkle Project. This innovative project will seek out members of the medical community to

support Rainforest Alliance programs. The alliance also supports the AMETRA 2001 project, which is a health center in Peru based on ethnobiology, or traditional medicines.

Rainforest Alliance will also continue to support other organizations in their efforts to save the rain forests and will work on developing sustainable practices for the tropical forests.

Membership Information and Volunteer Possibilities
Annual membership in the Rainforest Alliance is $20. There are reduced rates available for students and seniors. Members receive a subscription to the newsletter, *The Canopy*, along with a bimonthly schedule of events.

The alliance is a grassroots organization, and most of the programs are run by volunteers. Volunteer opportunities are available in several areas of the organization, including research, office work, and special projects and events. All members are encouraged to participate through a variety of ways: by organizing and attending benefit concerts, dinners, debates, or other similar events; by involving companies, schools, and local businesses in the rain forest cause; by encouraging teachers to use environmental curricula in the schools; by contacting local politicians, newspapers, and national leaders to voice opinions about policies; and by writing to international lenders to seek support for preservation and responsible development.

☐ RARE CENTER FOR TROPICAL BIRD CONSERVATION

19th and the Parkway
Philadelphia, PA 19103
(215) 299-1182
Contacts: George S. Glenn, Jr., Executive Director
James Newlin, Administrative Assistant

History/Goals
The RARE center was founded in 1973 and works on projects to directly aid the endangered tropical birds of the Caribbean and Latin America. The RARE center was originally called the Rare Animal Relief Effort until it changed its name in 1987.

Past Achievements
In 1974 the RARE center provided funding to help establish the Monteverde Cloud Forest Reserve in Costa Rica. RARE center also helped construct the original interpretive/research facility in the reserve.

The RARE center's research is utilized by many other organizations involved in the tropical rain forests. For instance, research on the endangered quetzal in the Monteverde reserve was utilized by the Monteverde Conservation League and Rainforest Alliance in a fund-raising campaign that brought in over $300,000 to secure critical parts of the quetzal habitats.

Ongoing Projects

In 1989, with a grant from The Pew Charitable Trusts, RARE center began the Design of Montane Parks program. This research and training program seeks revolutionary conservation ideas for tropical mountain areas.

One of RARE center's major ongoing projects is the Conservation Education for the Caribbean (CEC) program. The CEC program takes the issues of the rain forests to the local inhabitants of the country where a rain forest is located. Through songs, music videos, church sermons, billboards, bumper stickers, and school presentations, RARE center presents the plight of the rain forests to the locals. These programs have always been handled personally by the Caribbean Program Director, Paul Butler, but that limits RARE center to only one island each year. In 1989, however, RARE center began developing a training manual to enable local environmentalists to run the CEC program. The manual helps the local start by taking them through fifty-eight projects, to be done over a twelve-month period.

Future Plans

RARE center plans to study bird migration patterns at Monteverde and at the El Triunfo Biosphere Reserve in southern Mexico. RARE center will continue its education programs and its research programs in the Caribbean and Latin America.

Membership Information and Volunteer Possibilities

Membership in RARE Center for Tropical Bird Conservation is $30 annually. Members receive a copy of the annual report and periodic copies of special reports as they are published.

There are no specific volunteer programs within RARE center.

☐ RENEW AMERICA

1400 Sixteenth Street, NW, Suite 710
Washington, DC 20036
(202) 232-2252
Contacts: Kevin M. Honness, Administrative Assistant
Tina Hobson, Executive Director

History/Goals

Renew America was established as a clearinghouse for environmental information. The organization disseminates information and gives recommendations to policy makers, environmental organizations, and the media.

Past Achievements

Since its founding, Renew America has been collecting, organizing, and disseminating information in the form of reports, pamphlets, and books.

It has produced reports covering such topics as global warming, environmental dangers in rural America, and sustainable energy.

Ongoing Projects

One of Renew America's biggest projects is the annual *State of the States* report. The report, first published in 1987, is a state-by-state report card on environmental policies. Renew America cooperates with over 100 state and local environmental groups to release the *State of the States* report each year.

Future Plans

Renew America plans to continue its work as a clearinghouse of information for the environmental community. The *State of the States* report will continue to be published annually, along with other reports and books as research is completed.

Membership Information and Volunteer Possibilities

Annual membership in Renew America is $25. Members receive the quarterly *Renew America Report*, which keeps them up-to-date concerning the organization's work. Members also receive the annual *State of the States* report and 50 percent discounts on publications.

There are no formal volunteer positions available within the organization, although there are some internships available.

☐ RODALE INSTITUTE

222 Main Street
Emmaus, PA 18098
(215) 967-5171
Contacts: Robert D. Hart, Director
James O. Morgan, Vice President

History/Goals

The Rodale Institute was established to "advance the public well-being in the areas of food, health, and natural resources." Rodale reaches this goal through research, education, and practical action.

Past Achievements

The Rodale Institute has developed the 305-acre Rodale Research Center in Pennsylvania. This center is a research farm that tries out Rodale's philosophy of gardening and farming. During 1989 a bookstore was opened at the center in the Siegfreidale Schoolhouse. The bookstore also serves as the starting point for a self-guided tour of the center. During 1989 the institute held its first day-long GardenFest! This event attracted more than 400 people, who attended a soil health workshop and an insect management seminar, toured the center, and tasted fresh organic produce.

During 1989 Rodale established two new offices, the rural/urban office and the cooperative research office. The rural/urban office was established to address the increasing problems of farmers in areas fast becoming urban centers. The cooperative research office was established to facilitate cooperative efforts between scientists at the center and those at universities throughout the United States, at the U.S. Department of Agriculture, and at research institutions in Europe.

Ongoing Projects

The institute has several ongoing projects at the center: the new crops program, the horticulture program, the agronomy research program. The new crops program works to develop new drought-tolerant plants, and to help in soil conservation efforts or in other cropping systems. The horticulture program works to develop systems for gardens and orchards that produce pesticide-free vegetables, fruits, flowers, and herbs. The research garden, begun in 1974, continues to concentrate on the needs of the home gardener or small-scale fruit producer. Many of the projects conducted through the horticulture program are done in association with *Organic Gardening* magazine, published by Rodale Press. The agronomy research program seeks to develop crops that enhance the productiveness of the soil and other natural resources. The program works to establish systems that are productive over the long term, are environmentally sound, and are economically feasible. The program also seeks to present farmers and other agricultural professionals with alternatives to chemical farming.

Through the newly established cooperative research program, Rodale Research Center has established cooperative agreements with Pennsylvania State University, Cornell University, Michigan State University, University of Vermont, Rutgers University, University of Missouri, USDA, World Resources Institute, and World Neighbors. Internationally, Rodale has established cooperative agreements with University of Padova (Italy), Northeast Forestry University (China), South China Environmental Institute, Jiangsu Academy of Agricultural Sciences (China), and Institute for Land Improvement and Grassland Farming (Poland).

Another major project of the center is FONE, or Farmers' Own Network for Education. This is a network of several thousand farmers throughout the United States who participate in workshops, field days, and special forums, and use the network for sharing and exchanging ideas.

The institute also publishes many books and other sources of information. One of its largest publications is *The New Farm* magazine, available by subscription for $11.97 per year. In addition, to get information out to the public, the Rodale Institute sponsors community workshops. Many of the workshops are intended for farming communities or gardeners; there are also a number of youth workshops.

Rodale Institute has numerous international programs. The network of Regenerative Agriculture Resource Centers established an African site in Senegal in 1987. This is a community action program helping Senegalese workers and farmers become more aware of and able to utilize agricultural alternatives that are better for the ecosystem. This Senegalese RARC is the core of the institute's work in West Africa. The West African program is part of the International Information Exchange Network, which enables researchers and development workers worldwide to share research and other information and to help develop regenerative agricultural techniques. IIEN keeps the network informed through the use of a newsletter, *International Ag-Sieve*, and electronic telecommunications via CARINET and CGNET.

Future Plans

Rodale Institute will work to build up its two newest programs, the cooperative research program and the rural/urban program. Although numerous cooperative research agreements have already been established, Rodale will seek new agreements with additional universities and organizations.

Rodale also hopes to set up programs similar to the Regenerative Agriculture Resource Center in Senegal in countries such as Guatemala, Ecuador, and Kenya.

The institute will continue to publish research reports and other materials for the general public and for agriculture professionals.

Membership Information and Volunteer Possibilities

Annual membership in the Rodale Institute is $25, with a $15 membership available for students and seniors. Members receive the *Partner Report*, a quarterly newsletter.

Members can join the Community Regeneration Network and receive a bimonthly newsletter, *Regeneration*. The Community Regeneration Network is the volunteer, grassroots portion of the institute. This network focuses on community revitalization. Members of the network also receive environmental materials, educational materials, and other publications. The network presents workshops, makes presentations, and provides consulting services where necessary. The network has an extensive library of research and resource files and maintains a data base of activists at the local level.

☐ THE RUFFED GROUSE SOCIETY

1400 Lee Drive
Coraopolis, PA 15108
(412) 262-4044
Contacts: Samuel R. Pursglove, Jr., Executive Director
Mary Cowder, Director of Membership Services

History/Goals

The Ruffed Grouse Society was formed in 1961 by several ruffed grouse hunters. Today there are 20,000 members, with chapters in various states and in several Canadian provinces. The society's main goal is the improvement of the environment for the ruffed grouse, woodcock, and other forest wildlife by maintaining, improving, and expanding their habitats. Habitat improvement research money is channeled through an affiliated organization, the Forest Wildlife Foundation.

Past Achievements

One of the major events for the society each year is the Sportsmen's Banquets, held throughout the country at local chapters. In 1981 these dinners brought in a little over $450,000. In 1988 there were over 100 fund-raisers, bringing in over $1 million.

Ruffed grouse are frequently found in aspen groves across the country. To encourage the maintenance of this important habitat, the Ruffed Grouse Society's ruffed grouse management area program in the western Great Lakes region works to clear-cut the older stands of aspen to allow the necessary sunlight to reach the young trees. In 1987 the society became a partner with the U.S. Forest Service to promote more and better habitat for grouse and woodcock in national forests.

Ongoing Projects

The society publishes a number of booklets and guides focusing on the improvement of woodland habitat for wildlife. The society also sponsors seminars, symposiums, and conferences dealing with forest wildlife management.

The society sponsors habitat improvement demonstration areas that are made accessible to the public. The society also funds projects working to gain new information on forest wildlife management. The results from these studies are used to modify current forestry management programs.

Representatives from the society regularly give on-site consultations to landowners concerning habitat improvements.

Future Plans

The society plans to continue with the same goals it established in 1961 when it was founded. The organization hopes to continue expanding its support base and to continue with the cooperative habitat improvement projects it has begun on public lands.

Membership Information and Volunteer Possibilities

There is a minimum membership fee of $20 annually. Members receive a year's subscription to the quarterly magazine *RGS*, a copy of Gordon Gullion's pamphlet *The Ruffed Grouse*, and invitations to international, regional, and local meetings.

Volunteers are encouraged to become involved in state and local chapter activities. These include the formation of wildlife habitat improvement demonstration areas and the planning of fund-raising activities such as the Sportsmen's Banquet.

☐ SAVE-THE-REDWOODS LEAGUE

114 Sansome Street, Room 605
San Francisco, CA 94104
(415) 362-2352
Contacts: Bruce S. Howard, President
John B. Dewitt, Secretary and Executive Director

History/Goals

The Save-the-Redwoods League was founded in 1918 and has been purchasing redwood lands for public parks protection since then. Since its founding, league members have donated over $63 million, which has been used to purchase over 260,000 acres of redwood lands that are protected in the thirty-two California Redwood State Parks, Muir Woods National Monument, and Redwood and Sequoia national parks. The league continues in its mission to purchase redwood lands for public parks, thus preserving the Redwoods for present and future generations. There are currently 50,000 members in the Save-the-Redwoods League, coming from all over the United States.

Past Achievements

The league announced, in January 1990, the purchase of an additional 120 acres of land to be added to the Portola Redwoods State Park in San Mateo County, California. The land cost $536,000. Half of that amount was provided by the league; the other half was matched from state park bond funds. Portola Redwoods, established in 1945 when the state purchased an original 1,600-acre tract of land, is significant in that, in addition to the redwoods, it is the site of the Iverson cabin. The Iverson cabin was built in the 1860s by Christian Iverson, the first European settler of record in the area. The park now contains over 2,400 acres and adjoins the 7,000-acre Pescadero Creek County Park. Since 1977 the league has spent over $2 million protecting the Portola Redwoods State Park.

A settlement agreement was reached in the summer of 1990 between the Save-the-Redwoods League, the Sierra Club and other conservation groups, and the U.S. Forest Service concerning the giant sequoia groves in Sequoia National Forest. The settlement agreement stipulates that, for the ten-year life of the agreement, it is illegal to commercially log inside a giant sequoia grove. The league had also succeeded in saving two other giant sequoia groves, by helping establish the Calaveras Big Trees State Park in 1931 and by saving the South Grove and adding it to that park in 1952.

In 1906 Fort Ross State Historic Park was established seventy-five miles north of San Francisco. This fort was the site of the most permanent Russian settlement in California. In December 1989 the league acquired 2,100 acres from the Fibreboard Corporation to enlarge the park, extending it from the shoreline up to the ridgeline. This tripled the size of the park and protected the land, the view, and the watershed.

Ongoing Projects

The league's ongoing projects include rescuing areas of primeval forests; cooperating with the California State Park Commission, the National Park Service, and others in establishing redwood parks and various other parks; purchasing redwood groves; helping increase public understanding of the importance of the primeval redwood or sequoia and other American forests; and supporting reforestation and conservation in forests.

Future Plans

The league will continue to purchase land and to use the media to carry its message to the public. The league also occasionally publishes pamphlets designed to educate the public on the value of the ancient forests.

Membership Information and Volunteer Possibilities

Annual membership in the league is $10, and life memberships are available for $100. Members each receive two bulletins a year.

There are no formal volunteer opportunities within the Save-the-Redwoods League, but the national parks and other areas that the league works to preserve are open to the public.

☐ SEA SHEPHERD CONSERVATION SOCIETY

P.O. Box 7000-S
Redondo Beach, CA 90277
(213) 373-6979
Contact: Paul Watson, Founder

History/Goals

Sea Shepherd Conservation Society was founded in 1979 by Paul Watson. Mr. Watson, one of the founders of Greenpeace, broke from that group to take a more direct approach at saving endangered whales, dolphins, and seals. Unlike Greenpeace, Sea Shepherd believes in taking direct action against individuals and groups they believe are harming the animals. Sea Shepherd describes itself as a "policing body" with the task of enforcing international regulations against the illegal slaughter of whales, dolphins, and seals. According to Sea Shepherd, the group has earned the reputation of "samurai conservationists" in Japan.

Past Achievements

Sea Shepherd Conservation Society states that it has been responsible for sinking seven illegal whaling ships. In 1979 Sea Shepherd's boat, the *Sea Shepherd*, located the *Sierra*, a whaling ship owned by a South African businessman, off the coast of Portugal. The *Sea Shepherd* rammed the *Sierra*, causing it to go into harbor for repairs. While in the harbor in Portugal, the *Sierra* was sunk at dockside.

The next year Sea Shepherd sank two Spanish whalers, *Isba I* and *Isba II*, in a harbor in Spain. In 1986 Sea Shepherd engineers sank two of Iceland's four whaling ships and destroyed a whale processing factory in Iceland.

In 1983 Sea Shepherd blockaded the Canadian sealing fleet, keeping them from the ice fields off eastern Canada and away from the harp seals. Sea Shepherd claims to have saved 78,000 seals through the success of the blockade.

Through fund-raising efforts, Sea Shepherd has purchased two of the Orkney Islands off the Scottish coast and has turned the islands into sanctuaries where seals are protected.

Ongoing Activities

Sea Shepherd Conservation Society continues to fight for the survival of whales, dolphins, and seals. In an effort to increase public awareness of the plight of these marine animals, Sea Shepherd conducts educational programs. The group also continues to take direct action against any peoples or nations that it believes are harming the lives of these animals.

Future Plans

Sea Shepherd plans to continue to fight for the lives of dolphins, whales, and seals. They claim that four countries—Japan, Norway, Iceland, and the Soviet Union—currently violate regulations protecting whales. Sea Shepherd will continue to confront ships from these countries in an effort to stop the killing of whales.

The group also battles the drift net fishery, which Sea Shepherd claims causes the deaths of over 100,000 marine mammals and 1 million sea birds each year in the North Pacific. They have chased drift net fishing boats out of U.S. waters and have cut drift nets to free trapped whales and dolphins.

Membership Information and Volunteer Possibilities

Annual membership in Sea Shepherd Conservation Society is $25 and includes a subscription to the quarterly newsletter, *Sea Shepherd Log*.

Sea Shepherd is an all-volunteer organization, with no paid staff positions. The crew members on the boats that pursue whaling ships, blockade seal hunts, and attempt to interfere with drift net fishing are all volunteers.

☐ SIERRA CLUB

P.O. Box 7959
San Francisco, CA 94120–9943
(415) 776-2211
Contact: Michael L. Fischer, Executive Director

History/Goals

The Sierra Club was founded in 1892 by naturalist John Muir to help preserve the beauty of the Sierra Nevada range. Today there are nearly half a million members across the United States dedicated to preserving wilderness areas and protecting the natural environment.

Past Achievements

Throughout its history the Sierra Club has had a significant impact on the formation of America's national park and wilderness preservation systems. The Sierra Club claims to have helped preserve over 130 million acres of public land during its nearly hundred years of existence.

The Sierra Club has established fifty-seven chapters throughout the United States and has branch offices in Alaska; Maryland; Canada; Wisconsin; New York; Oakland and Los Angeles, California; Wyoming; Washington; Tennessee; Florida; Texas; Colorado; Utah; Arizona; and Washington, D.C.

The Sierra Club has published numerous books focusing on topics such as energy, environmental action, land use, public lands, pollution, population, international issues, water resources, wildlife, and outdoor activities.

Ongoing Projects

The Sierra Club is involved in numerous legislative activities such as lobbying, research, legal and policy development. The club also has an extensive publications department and frequently produces publications about current issues in the environmental struggle.

One of the Sierra Club's most well known services is the outing program. The Sierra Club sponsors approximately 270 trips annually that include national and international destinations. Trips within the United States range in price from $210 to approximately $900 and usually run for one week. Trips include such destinations as Ocala Forest, Florida; Glen Canyon Recreation Area, Utah; Galiuro Wilderness, Arizona; Grand Canyon, Arizona; Cranberry Wilderness, West Virginia; Zion Park and Arch Canyon, Utah; Virgin Islands Park, Virgin Islands; Louisiana and Mississippi; Anza-Borrego Park, California; and family trips at Everglades Park, Florida. International trips include destinations such as Annapurna Sanctuary, Nepal; Rajasthan Desert Kingdoms, India; a study and walking tour through China; cross-country skiing in Austria; Dartmoor and Exmoor Parks, England; Italy; Scotland; Germany and Switzerland; Costa Rica; Guatemala; Belize; whale watching in Magdalena Bay, Baja California, Mexico; the east Caribbean; Brazil's Amazon Basin; Patagonia and Tierra del Fuego, Argentina; New Zealand; Australia; the Soviet Union; and the Silk Road across China and the Soviet Union. Trips run for one to three weeks and range in price from $1,950 to $3,725.

The Sierra Club has established the Earthcare Network as an informal group of organizations that can work together on major campaigns. The network helps to generate publicity and to mobilize grassroots support from all organizations. The network also provides information on international campaigns and will track down hard-to-find information. The network will promote exchanges between international groups as well as "sister city" relationships between groups in the United States and abroad.

Future Plans

The Sierra Club plans to preserve additional wilderness areas throughout the United States. The club will also continue its efforts to work toward a healthy environment by trying to restrict pesticides and to clean up toxic wastes. Some of the key issues for the future will be the global environment, acid rain, water and air pollution, hazardous wastes, ozone depletion, and global warming.

Membership Information and Volunteer Possibilities

Annual membership in the Sierra Club is $33, or $41 for a joint membership. There are reduced rates of $15 available for seniors, students, and those on limited incomes, and lifetime memberships for $750. Members receive a subscription to *Sierra*, the quarterly magazine. Members also receive special discounts on books and calendars and are eligible to take the Sierra Club outings. Each member belongs to one of the local chapters and will receive chapter publications and invitations to local trips and events. Members also elect local leaders and the board of directors.

There are numerous volunteer possibilities through the local chapters. The Sierra Club has published a series of guides for activists who want advice on topics such as tropical rain forests, solving the garbage crisis, stabilizing world population, and protecting the coasts from offshore oil development. The Sierra Club is a grassroots organization, so many activities through the chapters are ongoing. There are over 350 volunteer groups throughout the United States whose activities include lobbying, research, information, letter writing, and organizing campaigns.

☐ SIERRA CLUB LEGAL DEFENSE FUND

2044 Fillmore Street
San Francisco, CA 94115
(415) 567-6100
Contacts: Fredric P. Sutherland, Executive Director
Joanna C. Chestnut, Administrator

History/Goals

The Sierra Club Legal Defense Fund is known as "the law firm of the environmental movement." The Legal Defense Fund works closely with the Sierra Club but is a wholly independent organization. Founded in 1971 the Legal Defense Fund provides legal services to the environmental movement. There are twenty-eight staff attorneys for the Legal Defense Fund located in offices in San Francisco, Washington, D.C., Denver,

Juneau, Seattle, and Honolulu. The Legal Defense Fund has over 80,000 supporters and has represented nearly every major conservation organization as well as numerous smaller groups.

Past Achievements

The Sierra Club Legal Defense Fund has been successful in numerous lawsuits. In Mineral King Valley, California, the Legal Defense Fund stopped construction of a ski resort until the valley was added to Sequoia National Park. The construction of a supertanker port was stopped in Galveston Bay, Texas. In Kaiparowits Plateau, Utah, the construction of the world's largest coal-fired power plant was stopped. In Little Granite Creek, Wyoming, the Legal Defense Fund held back oil and gas drilling projects proposed by then-Interior Secretary James Watt until the area could be included in the Gros Ventre Wilderness Area.

The Legal Defense Fund forced the EPA to halt the production and use of chlordane in the United States. Burning of toxic and radioactive wastes was stopped at the Rocky Flats nuclear weapons plant near Denver, Colorado. Another lawsuit established the federal government's right to claim water rights over the interests of agriculture and industry when necessary to preserve enough free-flowing water to maintain plant and animal life on public lands.

The Legal Defense Fund has won cases aimed at preserving numerous wildlife species, including grizzlies, palilas, whooping cranes, fur seals, Dall's porpoises, and red-cockaded woodpeckers.

Ongoing Projects

The Sierra Club Legal Defense Fund continually represents environmental organizations and provides legal services to organizations. Some of the current focuses include fighting to stop open pit mining and clear-cut logging in Misty Fjords and Admiralty Island national monuments, Alaska; strengthening the Clean Air Act and working to improve the air quality in cities such as Denver, Los Angeles, San Francisco, Houston, Chicago, and New York.

A lawsuit filed in 1990 on behalf of the North Cascades Conservation Council attempts to protect the North Cascades National Park and the Ross Lake and Lake Chelan national recreation areas from development and clear-cutting.

Future Plans

The Sierra Club Legal Defense Fund will continue its representation of the environmental movement. It will continue to use litigation in an effort to protect the environment.

Membership Information and Volunteer Possibilities

There is no formal membership in the Sierra Club Legal Defense Fund, but rather a network of supporters. For a minimum $10 contribution annually, supporters receive a subscription to the quarterly newsletter, *In Brief*, along with updates and other information. There are no formal volunteer possibilities within the organization. There are, however, a number of legal internships available annually.

☐ UNION OF CONCERNED SCIENTISTS

26 Church Street
Cambridge, MA 02238
(617) 547-5552
Contact: Elizabeth Geer, Public Information Assistant
Howard Rix, Executive Director

History/Goals

The Union of Concerned Scientists was founded in 1969 by a group of students and faculty members at Massachusetts Institute of Technology. Today there are over 100,000 members and a staff of thirty divided between the home office and the Washington, D.C., office. UCS has four basic goals: nuclear arms reduction; a sensible and stable national security policy; nuclear power safety; and a sound energy policy for the United States. These goals are accomplished through research, public education, lobbying, and litigation. UCS is also a member of the Environmental Federation of America.

Past Achievements

The Union of Concerned Scientists took the first public look at the nuclear power industry in 1971 through the 1971 Atomic Energy Commission hearings. These hearings revealed for the first time the major weaknesses in nuclear plant system designs.

Between 1981 and 1988 UCS held an Annual Week of Education on the nuclear arms race at universities all across the country.

During 1989 UCS conducted a Voter Education Project. The project resulted in the production of a one-hour prime-time television special in conjunction with the Better World Society. "Mandate from Main Street: Americans Advise the Next President" was seen by close to two million viewers over the Turner Broadcasting System in the United States and on nationwide TV in the Soviet Union.

In early 1989 UCS and the Council on Economic Priorities, the Sierra Club, the Natural Resources Defense Council, Physicians for Social Responsibility, and International Physicians for the Prevention of Nuclear War sponsored an International Scientific Symposium on a Nuclear Test Ban. The conference was attended by over 600 grassroots activists from across the country.

In 1977 over 12,000 scientists signed the UCS-sponsored "Scientists' Declaration on the Nuclear Arms Race," which urged a halt to underground testing and a moratorium on testing and deployment of new nuclear weapons.

In 1984 UCS released a study, which later was developed into the book *The Fallacy of Star Wars*, describing the technical flaws, the enormous costs, and other implications of the Strategic Defense Initiative.

UCS has developed video conferences, television documentaries, and advocacy videos, along with the first junior high school curriculum on nuclear war and arms control issues.

Ongoing Projects

The Union of Concerned Scientists is continually producing educational videos on global warming and energy options. UCS conducts national lobbying efforts aimed at advancing efficient energy options and developing renewable-energy technologies.

The Week of Education, held annually during the 1980s and focusing on the nuclear arms race, now focuses on global warming. The education week, conducted at hundreds of universities, consists of panel discussions, lectures, debates, films, exhibits, and other educational events. UCS supplies educators with organizing materials, program suggestions, background information, and educational resources.

UCS conducts oversight and analysis of the Nuclear Regulatory Commission on an ongoing basis.

UCS has established a lobbying and litigation program on Capitol Hill. This group of experts lobbies Congress, provides expert testimony to congressional committees, and participates in several legislative coalitions.

Future Plans

The Union of Concerned Scientists will continue to focus on the issues of energy strategies and defense policies through research, education, lobbying, and litigation. UCS will continue to hold the Annual Education Week and to publish books, papers, videos, and curricula for schools and universities.

Membership Information and Volunteer Possibilities

Annual membership in the Union of Concerned Scientists is $20. Members, called "sponsors," receive the quarterly journal, *Nucleus*.

There are several areas for volunteers within the organization. The Scientists' Action Network is a group of over 12,000 scientists who work on education and lobbying programs at the local levels. The Legislative Alert Network keeps all sponsors informed of upcoming congressional votes. Sponsors are then encouraged to write letters and make phone calls to representatives and senators. The Professionals' Coalition for Nuclear Arms Control is a network of UCS scientists who work with physicians, lawyers, and design professionals in communities across the United States on arms control education and legislation.

☐ UNITED STATES PUBLIC INTEREST RESEARCH GROUP

215 Pennsylvania Avenue, SE
Washington, DC 20003
(202) 546-9707
Contacts: Gene Karpinski, Executive Director
Nancy E. Griffin, Administrative Assistant

History/Goals
The U.S. Public Interest Research Group was established in 1983 as a national lobbying office for state PIRGs. U.S. PIRG conducts research and lobbies for consumer and environmental protection.

Past Achievements
In 1986 U.S. PIRG helped lead the campaign that led to the strengthening of the Superfund, a $9 billion toxic waste cleanup program.

Also in 1986 U.S. PIRG helped gain passage of the Safe Drinking Water Act. This act requires that water supplies be more thoroughly and frequently tested, for a wider range of chemical contaminants, than was done previously.

The 1987 Clean Water Act was also strengthened through the efforts of U.S. PIRG and other environmental organizations. The new act provides for the cleanup and protection of major waterways in the United States.

The state PIRGs have also brought about changes in environmental policy. The New Jersey PIRG was victorious in 1990 when the New Jersey Legislature passed the Clean Water Enforcement Act. Polluters in New Jersey will receive mandatory and automatic fines.

State PIRGs combined have won over forty Clean Water Act enforcement lawsuits against various polluters, resulting in over $12 million in penalties.

Ongoing Projects
U.S. PIRG focuses on seven major areas: clean air, consumer rights, toxic waste cleanup, atmospheric protection, pesticide control, solid waste reduction and recycling, and open government. U.S. PIRG works for swift cleanup of toxic wastes and calls for the polluters to pay all costs of the cleanup. U.S. PIRG calls for reduced carbon dioxide emissions through greater energy efficiency and through the use of renewable energy sources. U.S. PIRG has lobbyists in Washington who work on the passage of bills to ban carcinogenic pesticides from food and to prevent groundwater contamination. U.S. PIRG also works to reduce, recycle, and reuse the trash in this country. Lobbyists work on the passage of legislation to reduce unnecessary packaging, to pass a national bottle bill, and to halt all garbage incineration.

Future Plans

U.S. PIRG is calling for action in the near future to drastically cut acid rain-causing pollutants, to enact stronger auto emissions standards, and to tighten the limits placed on toxic air pollutants emitted by such sources as chemical plants and automobiles.

U.S. PIRG will be continuing work in the future on gaining passage of legislation to require cleaner fuels, to mandate alternative fuels, and to work on getting nonpolluting buses in the country's twenty-seven smoggiest cities.

Membership Information and Volunteer Possibilities

Membership in U.S. PIRG is $25 annually. Membership fees and donations are used to pay the research, lobbying, and organizing staff at the national office. Members receive *U.S. PIRG Citizen Agenda*, the quarterly newsletter. Each newsletter contains investigative reports, updates on state campaigns, reports on legislative votes, and staff profiles.

Volunteers are welcomed in U.S. PIRG. There are state PIRGs, which do work at the state and local levels and regularly utilize volunteers in their grassroots campaigns. Members are also encouraged to write or call the president, Senate leaders, and House members when certain votes are expected. Other campaigns also get members involved, such as the recent campaign calling for members to send aluminum cans to members of Congress in an effort to encourage a national bottle bill.

☐ WATERFOWL U.S.A., LIMITED

Box 50, The Waterfowl Building
Edgefield, SC 29824
(803) 637-5767
Contact: Roger White, Executive Vice President

History/Goals

Waterfowl U.S.A. Limited is an organization consisting of state and local chapters that raise funds to provide a future for America's waterfowl. Waterfowl U.S.A. is primarily an organization of hunters and other outdoor sports enthusiasts. The group's motto is "American Bucks for American Ducks."

Waterfowl U.S.A.'s major goals are to stimulate an interest in preserving the remaining waterfowl wetland habitat in the United States; to organize a network of local groups made up of biologists, sportsmen, and bird enthusiasts; to educate the public on waterfowl and waterfowl habitat preservation; and to educate children on sound conservation practices.

Past Achievements

Waterfowl U.S.A. has worked with groups of Boy Scouts all over the country on wildlife management programs.

The organization has worked on placing nesting boxes and food in several areas of the country to support duck populations.

The Northwest Indiana Chapter of Waterfowl U.S.A. donated $8,000 to the Indiana Department of Natural Resources in 1989 for wetland acquisition in the state of Indiana.

Ongoing Projects

One of Waterfowl U.S.A.'s major ongoing projects is the annual "Waterfowlers' Outdoor Adventure Sweepstakes." The winner of the annual sweepstakes receives an all-expense-paid trip to the Texas Gulf Coast, Louisiana, or Arkansas to hunt with a movie star or sports celebrity.

Waterfowl U.S.A.'s chapters also work on projects to build refuges, dike wetlands, band birds, build nest structures, and preserve waterfowl areas. The organization also works with various youth organizations to educate them on waterfowl and waterfowl habitat.

Future Plans

Many of the local chapters have plans for the future. The Wisconsin chapter recently began raising money to buy a marsh to provide a private area to plant feed for waterfowl. The Illinois Bald Cypress Chapter has been working with the Nature Conservancy and Ducks Unlimited to get a 35,000-acre refuge established on the lower Cash River in Illinois.

Membership Information and Volunteer Possibilities

Annual basic membership in Waterfowl U.S.A. is $15. Members receive a waterfowler's wristwatch, an official duck and goose band, a duck call, and a subscription to the bimonthly magazine, *Waterfowl*. Charter membership is $25 annually and entitles members to the additional gift of a waterfowl print. For $200 annually, sponsor members receive a plaque at the National Headquarters, a stamp print, a limited edition decoy, a pewter pin, a 24k gold-plated wristwatch, and the other benefits of basic membership. There are also $1,000 life memberships available.

Volunteer opportunities exist through the local chapters. Local chapters have fund-raising banquets and other events, work in conservation projects at the local level, and help to publicize the organization. Members are also encouraged to start local chapters in areas where none exist.

☐ WHITETAILS UNLIMITED

P.O. Box 422
Sturgeon Bay, WI 54235
(414) 743-6777
Contact: Peter J. Gerl, Chief Executive Officer

History/Goals

Whitetails Unlimited was founded in 1982 to instruct hunters and non-hunters about sound deer management in the United States. The organization sponsors a wide range of activities, from conservation scholarships to habitat redevelopment programs.

Past Achievements

Since its founding, WTU has started over ninety local chapters throughout the United States. The organization has developed a kit that can be used by interested people at the local level to start a local chapter.

Ongoing Projects

Whitetails Unlimited carries out three basic programs: a public awareness program to bring information on the White-tailed deer and its habitat to the public's attention and to educate the public on improving the management of the deer; a research program to increase understanding of biological and cultural problems affecting the white-tailed deer; and a telecommunication and data base system, which is currently in the planning stage.

To increase public awareness of the white-tailed deer, WTU sponsors seminars and trade shows, makes public announcements, distributes educational brochures, pamphlets, and booklets, and offers various teaching aids for the classroom.

To increase the research efforts aimed at the white-tailed deer, WTU financially supports research in federal and state fish and wildlife departments and at universities and laboratories.

Future Plans

Whitetails Unlimited is working on indexing information on the white-tailed deer through a telecommunication network and computer data base. WTU plans to index information available at all educational levels as well as to index and provide materials to the general public. WTU hopes to be a central source of information on the white-tailed deer to agencies and organizations across the United States.

WTU hopes to launch a public awareness campaign that will successfully address these problems: improve landuser/landowner relations; combat poaching; improve the image of hunters and other outdoor sports enthusiasts; reduce deer/vehicle collisions; reduce crop depredation; improve wildlife habitat; promote regulated hunting as a management tool; and increase hunter education.

Membership Information and Volunteer Possibilities

Annual membership in Whitetails Unlimited is $15. Junior membership for those under twelve years is available for $5, and life memberships are $200. Members receive a subscription to *The Deer Trail* magazine and have access to the WTU video library. Members can also participate in the annual photo contest, the trophy buck award program, the successful deer hunter award program, and the membership harvest forum. Members receive discounts on WTU merchandise and are notified of any new products. Individual chapters also sponsor banquets and offer membership incentives.

Volunteers are encouraged to utilize the chapter kit and establish a local chapter of WTU. WTU has the aspiration of "taking the dedication and overall sportsmen's attitude associated with the number one big game animal in the United States, the white-tailed deer, and channeling it into useful volunteer efforts." Most of these volunteer efforts are at the local level.

☐ THE WILDERNESS SOCIETY
900 Seventeenth Street, NW
Washington, DC 20006-2596
(202) 833-2300
Contact: George T. Frampton, Jr., President

History/Goals
The Wilderness Society was founded in 1935 and is devoted to the preservation of wilderness and wildlife. The society works to protect America's forests, parks, rivers, deserts, and shorelands. There are currently close to 350,000 members nationwide, with a staff of 135 and fifteen field offices throughout the United States.

Past Achievements
In 1976 The Wilderness Society and concerned citizens were able to persuade Congress to require the Bureau of Land Management to publicly identify all of the lands it held that had no roads and to make recommendations concerning those lands to be preserved for wilderness areas.

In 1989 the society successfully campaigned for the enactment of tougher oil-spill liability legislation as a result of the Exxon Valdez oil spill in Alaska's Prince William Sound.

After several years of work on the part of the Florida regional office, the society was gratified in 1989 when the Everglades National Park Protection and Expansion Act passed Congress. The act adds 110,000 acres of the East Everglades to the Everglades National Park and makes plans for the Army Corps of Engineers to modify the South Florida canal system to restore a natural water flow into the park.

Another 1989 legislative victory for The Wilderness Society was the passage of the Nevada Wilderness Protection Act of 1989. This act sets aside 733,400 acres of wilderness in the Humboldt and Toiyabe national forests, plus the Nevada portion of the Inyo. The act also opens up 2.4 million additional acres of national forest to multiple uses.

Ongoing Projects
For several years The Wilderness Society has worked to protect the Tongass National Forest in southeast Alaska. In 1988 a field office was opened in Juneau, Alaska, to help facilitate cooperation between the society and area residents working toward protection of the Tongass.

The project will continue until the society determines that the area is protected.

The Wilderness Society is working to secure wilderness designation for 17 million acres in Utah, New Mexico, Arizona, and California. The society is also working to save wildlands in Idaho, Montana, Nevada, Oregon, and Colorado.

The Wilderness Society works to reduce the amount of road building undertaken by the U.S. Forest Service, and seeks at the congressional level to reduce the funds available for the building of such roads. The society is also working on a legislative package of Forest Service reforms.

The Wilderness Society has established model national park protection projects at Yellowstone, the Everglades, and the Southern Appalachian Highlands, which include Great Smoky Mountains National Park. The society works to see that entire ecosystems are protected within wilderness areas.

Future Plans

The Wilderness Society's two top priorities for wildlife refuges in the future are: the education of the public and Congress about the need for consistent usage standards for refuges, and to stop oil drilling on the Arctic Wildlife Refuge's Coastal Plain.

The Wilderness Society has launched a campaign that will go for many years, working to save the ancient forests. This campaign involves research, public education, the establishment of biological data bases, mapping the forests, lobbying in Congress, negotiating with the Forest Service, and taking court actions to stop logging.

Membership Information and Volunteer Possibilities

Annual membership in The Wilderness Society is $30. Students and senior citizens can become members for $15 annually. Members receive a subscription to *Wilderness*, the quarterly magazine. There are no formal volunteer positions within the organization, as most activities are performed at the legislative levels by paid employees.

☐ THE WILDLIFE SOCIETY

5410 Grosvenor Lane
Bethesda, MD 20814
(301) 897-9770
Contact: Harry E. Hodgdon, Executive Director

History/Goals

The Wildlife Society is an organization of 8,500 members from over forty countries. Most of these members are professionals in the fields of resource management, such as wildlife ecology, although there are members from outside the profession who are interested in resource conservation and wildlife management.

Founded in Washington, D.C., in 1936 as The Society of Wildlife Specialists, The Wildlife Society was born one year later in St. Louis, Missouri. The society today has four principal objectives: sound stewardship of wildlife resources and the environment; the active prevention of the degradation of the environment by humans; an increase in the awareness and appreciation of wildlife; and high standards in the field of wildlife management.

Past Achievements

The society has served as a forum for wildlife managers for over fifty years, where ideas are discussed, solutions are formulated, and interaction with the public is encouraged.

In 1965 the first Student Wildlife Conclave of the Wildlife Society was formed. These conclaves were created by college and university students as forums where information, ideas, and comraderie could be exchanged. The conclaves still exist, and today there are four Student Wildlife Conclaves: Western, Central, Eastern, and Southeastern. The conclaves conduct seminars, feature guest speakers, arrange field trips, and sponsor wildlife quiz bowls.

Ongoing Projects

One of the society's strongest features is its publications. The quarterly *Journal of Wildlife Management* and *Wildlife Society Bulletin* are both major sources of scientific information for professionals, students, and educators. In addition, the Wildlife Monographs are a series of detailed, single-topic papers covering specific issues.

The society is a member of the International Union for Conservation of Nature and Natural Resources. The International Affairs Committee, one of thirty committees set up to address specific topics, actively participates in the International Congress of Game Biologists.

The society annually recognizes outstanding achievements in the wildlife field with several prestigious awards. The Aldo Leopold Memorial Award is the most famous of a number of such awards, given in recognition of distinguished service to wildlife conservation.

The Wildlife Society has a certification program designed to offer the public, employers, and clients access to wildlife management professionals who can provide accurate and reliable information on wildlife questions. A wildlife professional can be certified at one of two levels by the society: as a Certified Wildlife Biologist (who combines education and experience) or an Associate Wildlife Biologist (who has the necessary education but is still in the early stages of a professional career).

Future Plans

The society's work and publications are ongoing. Greater understanding between the public and wildlife managers is promoted. Programs and services are brought to the members through an ongoing series of conferences, workshops, and meetings.

Membership Information and Volunteer Possibilities
Annual membership in The Wildlife Society entitles members to receive
the bimonthly newsletter, *The Wildlifer*. Student memberships are also
available. The society also publishes two additional publications, available
to members for an extra fee: *Wildlife Society Bulletin* and *The Journal of
Wildlife Management*.

A continuing education program is available to members who are
wildlife professionals. Activities are also available through the Student
Wildlife Conclaves and the seven regional groups located throughout the
United States.

☐ WORLD SOCIETY FOR THE PROTECTION OF ANIMALS

29 Perkins Street,
P.O. Box 190
Boston, MA 02130
(617) 522-7000
Contact: John A. Hoyt, President

History/Goals
The World Society for the Protection of Animals, headquartered in
London with offices in six other countries, is an international disaster-
relief organization for animals. John Walsh, regional director of the
Western Hemisphere office, has been with the organization since its
beginning. Walsh joined the International Society for the Protection of
Animals nearly thirty years ago, just after its founding in 1959. In 1981
ISPA merged with the World Federation for the Protection of Animals,
which had been formed in 1950, to become WSPA. The office in
Massachusetts is responsible for all Western Hemisphere activities. WSPA
works with over 300 member societies in sixty-three countries throughout the world. The major goal of WSPA is to relieve the suffering of
animals worldwide, specifically during and after natural disasters.
Past Achievements
WSPA works with member societies from all over the world to form an
enormous animal protection network. When Panama's rain forests
flooded, WSPA saved over 4,000 animals. A voluntary animal sterilization
program was established in South and Central America. This sterilization
program has helped prevent the routine poisoning of thousands of
unwanted domestic animals and has helped control the stray dog population. The annual animal stoning festival in Spain was stopped with the
aid of WSPA.
Ongoing Projects
WSPA is working to stop the brutal treatment of dogs and cats used for
human consumption in Korea and the Philippines. When volcanic mud

washed over the Armero region in Colombia, WSPA treated pets and livestock and restored them to health. WSPA Kindness Clubs teach compassion for animals to children all over Africa.

Ongoing consumer information campaigns seek to inform the public about the suffering of animals. WSPA has been granted official nongovernmental organization consultative status at the United Nations. In that capacity, the society lobbies governments to introduce new legislation and to take the necessary steps to ensure that existing controls are properly observed and enforced.

Future Plans

The World Society for the Protection of Animals maintains a fund to help animals caught in natural disasters. The WSPA sponsors the World Congress for Animal Protection every six years; the next planned Congress is in 1996.

Membership Information and Volunteer Possibilities

Annual membership in the society is $20. Family memberships are available for $40 and life memberships for $500. Members receive the quarterly magazine, *Animals International*.

☐ THE WORLDWATCH INSTITUTE

1776 Massachusetts Avenue, NW
Washington, DC 20036
(202) 452-1999
Contact: Lester R. Brown, President

History/Goals

The Worldwatch Institute, based in Washington, D.C., was founded in 1975. The institute's major goal is to inform the public and policy makers about the relationship between the world economy and environmental issues. The research staff at Worldwatch Institute analyzes issues from a global perspective. The chairman of the board is former Secretary of Agriculture Orville Freeman, and the director of research and president is Lester R. Brown.

Past Achievements

Worldwatch Institute is the publisher of *State of the World*, an annual guide for environmentalists, government officials, business leaders, development specialists, journalists, economists, professors, students, and the concerned public. Annual sales in recent years have reached 200,000, and the guide was printed in Arabic, Chinese, French, German, Indonesian, Italian, Japanese, Polish, Portuguese, Spanish, and Russian in addition to English.

The institute, in a joint effort with the producers of the "Nova" series at WGBH-TV in Boston, brought a ten-part series based on *State of the World* to public television in the fall of 1990.

Ongoing Projects

Worldwatch Institute continues to publish *State of the World* annually, looking at issues such as global warming, water, agriculture, oceans, air quality, energy, and society as a whole.

State of the World is used as a textbook in over 900 courses at close to 600 universities in the United States, and excerpts have been published in magazines and journals all over the world.

Future Plans

Lester R. Brown stated he believes that the "nineties may be our last chance to reverse the trends that are undermining the human prospect. If we fail, environmental deterioration and economic decline may begin to feed on each other, making an effective response to these threats impossible. Effective action depends on reliable information. That's what *State of the World* is all about." Worldwatch Institute will continue with this goal into the 1990s and will continue to publish this text.

Membership Information and Volunteer Possibilities

Membership in the Worldwatch Library is $25 annually. This entitles members to a paperback edition of *State of the World* and all Worldwatch Papers released during a one-year period. Copies of the book are available without a membership.

Worldwatch Institute is not a grassroots volunteer organization. The institute serves its members through its publications, and members can become informed about environmental issues, thus allowing them to take a more active part in their personal lives, not directly through the institute.

☐ WORLD WILDLIFE FUND

1250 Twenty-fourth Street, NW
Washington, DC 20037
(202) 293-4800
Contact: Kathryn S. Fuller, President

History/Goals

The World Wildlife Fund was founded in 1961 to protect endangered wildlife and wildlands.

WWF is headquartered in Washington, D.C., and has over 900,000 members nationwide, making it the third largest environmental organization in the United States. The organization currently has an annual budget exceeding $35 million. WWF is affiliated with the international WWF network, which includes organizations in twenty-three countries and a home office in Gland, Switzerland.

In 1985 World Wildlife Fund became officially affiliated with The Conservation Foundation, an environmental policy research institute founded in 1948.

The World Wildlife Fund has set up a list of nine goals which it works to fulfill: to protect habitat; to protect individual species; to promote ecologically sound development; to support scientific investigation; to promote education in developing countries; to provide training for local wildlife professionals; to encourage self-sufficiency in developing countries; to monitor international wildlife trade; and to influence public opinion and the policies of governments and private institutions.

Past Achievements

Since its founding, WWF has implemented over 1,600 projects in more than 100 countries. During the 1980s over half of the program expenditures were used on over 500 programs in Latin America, including Manu National Park in Peru. Within this park's 6,000 square miles, nearly 10 percent of all bird species on earth are sheltered. WWF has also helped create nearly 200 national parks and preserves around the world, in places such as Kenya, Peru, and Nepal.

Ongoing Projects

One of WWF's major programs is TRAFFIC. This program monitors the international trade of wild animals and plants. The program is designed to pressure governments into curbing illegal trade and carefully monitoring lawful trade levels.

WWF works through the Wildlands and Human Needs Program, partially funded by the U.S. Agency for International Development, to support projects in Latin America, the Caribbean, Africa, and Asia. These projects are designed to provide economically viable alternatives to meeting development needs of local populations while ensuring the safety of the environment.

Future Plans

Asia's tropical forests and wildlands are a new priority for WWF. According to World Wildlife Fund, projects are being designed and implemented in several "biologically important" countries, including Nepal, Thailand, Bhutan, and Indonesia.

Membership Information and Volunteer Possibilities

World Wildlife Fund International is the largest international conservation organization in the world. Each membership in World Wildlife Fund (USA) costs $15 annually. Although there is no organized member involvement at the grassroots level, the membership brochure states that membership contributions are used immediately to "rescue endangered animals from extinction, defend the borders of national parks and reserves, curb illegal trade in rare species, train local park rangers and antipoaching teams, and help local peoples develop alternatives to destroying their natural heritage."

WWF receives approximately 69 percent of its revenues from individuals and spends approximately 85 percent of total revenues on programs.

☐ ZERO POPULATION GROWTH

1400 Sixteenth Street, NW, Suite 320
Washington, DC 20036
(202) 332-2200
Contacts: Dianne Sherman, Communications Director
Susan Weber, Executive Director

History/Goals
Zero Population Growth was founded by Paul R. Ehrlich to focus on the
need for a balance between the earth's population, environment, and
resources. ZPG works to ensure that the right to choose whether or not
to have children is an educated and responsible choice and that the
necessary means to those ends are available. ZPG works to safeguard
such things as population education, voluntary family planning, and the
right to choose an abortion. ZPG currently has over 25,000 members.

Past Achievements
Zero Population Growth's founder, Paul Ehrlich, coauthored the book
The Population Explosion, which explores some of the key issues of
ZPG's philosophy.

During the 1989 Combined Federal Campaign, ZPG earned close to
$90,000 and gained over 500 new members. ZPG plans to continue this
program each year.

Ongoing Projects
Zero Population Growth publishes reports throughout the year. Most
publications are free and include titles such as "Abortion in America,"
"Combating Teen Pregnancy: An Introductory Guide to Programs and
Resources," and various fact sheets that provide an overview of the
environmental, social, and economic ramifications of population
growth. Current fact sheets include: Airborne Poisons, Traffic Conges-
tion, The Garbage Crisis, Population and the Greenhouse Effect, World
Hunger, Recycling, Deforestation, Loss of Wildlife, and Water Wars.

ZPG has several education programs designed for the classroom. For
those in grades six through ten, there is "For Earth's Sake Teaching Kit."
This kit introduces students to the relationship between population and
the environment and includes activity modules, teacher's guide, population data sheet, resource list and a list of ways for individuals to help.
For secondary students, there is the "Global 2000 Countdown Kit,"
which includes fourteen modules and resources. The "USA by Numbers
Teaching Kit" consists of hands-on activities that help develop skills in
critical thinking, deductive reasoning, chart reading, data interpretation,
graphing, and communication at all levels.

ZPG also works to pressure the World Bank and White House officials
to consider population policies in devising international development
strategies. ZPG works at the congressional level to encourage the protec-

tion of reproductive freedoms, to expand birth control services, and to invest in new contraceptive technology.

Future Plans

ZPG plans to strengthen its work at the grassroots level to increase public awareness of population issues. ZPG will also continue to focus on issues such as urbanization and local growth, global warming, sustainability, transportation, family planning, and the fast-changing issues of immigration, population, and foreign aid legislation.

Membership Information and Volunteer Possibilities

Annual Membership in ZPG is $20, with reduced memberships for students and seniors. Members receive a one-year subscription to the *ZPG Reporter* and a 20 percent discount on publications and gifts from ZPG.

ZPG depends heavily on volunteers at the local level. Volunteers can become involved in three organized programs: Action Alert Network, Roving Reporter, and Growthbusters.

A GUIDE TO PERSONAL INVOLVEMENT

Many people often wonder what any one individual can do to help the environment. There is much that can be done, but it may take some thought before you discover exactly how you want to help.

As becomes evident after looking at a few of the organizations in the *Directory,* environmental organizations vary considerably. The first thing you, as an individual, must do is set your own goals. What do you want to accomplish; what are your priorities? As much as some of us would rather not, we must limit our focus; an individual cannot solve every problem. Once you have determined your own expectations, you can look at each organization and determine which ones are most closely matched to your own interests.

How do the various organizations actually differ? The organizations in the *Directory* are national organizations; there may be other state and local organizations you would prefer to contact. Many organizations are national or international in scope, with local chapters or affiliates across the country. Many of the national organizations can put you in touch with local representatives. More and more common are the coalitions being formed by various groups. For instance, the Greater Yellowstone Coalition is made up of a large number of national and local organizations. Some members of this particular coalition, such as Environmental Defense Fund and The Wildlife Society, generally have a much broader scope but have chosen to focus one segment of their work on this particular issue.

While some organizations focus on many issues (such as World Wildlife Fund, The Nature Conservancy, Environmental Defense Fund, Natural Resources Defense Council, The Wilderness Society), there are others that focus only on a single issue (Rainforest Action Network, National Toxics Campaign, Desert Bighorn Council, Save-the-Redwoods League). Some organizations conduct research, litigate or lobby for their programs, run educational programs, and publish books and reports;

others are direct-action groups. For example, Earth First! and Sea Shepherds are aggressive, sometimes controversial groups whose actions attract considerable media attention. Others, such as Greenpeace, are direct-action groups who protest negative policies and often work on dangerous projects while staying just inside the law. Still other groups involve members in letter writing, boycotts, lobbying, door-to-door campaigns, and demonstrations. How much or how little you become involved depends on your own preferences and the organizations you choose to support. It is also helpful to notice how the organization spends its money, and who supports the group, before making a final choice.

In addition to the nonprofit and other private environmental organizations, there are other places to become involved in working for the environment. Many government agencies, including the U.S. Forest Service, the Soil Conservation Service, and the Bureau of Land Management, utilize volunteers in many of their programs. A bimonthly magazine, *Buzzworm: The Environmental Journal*, includes a six- to eight-page section titled "Connections" in each issue. This section lists volunteer positions and environmental jobs available throughout the country. There are also several newsletters currently available that advertise environmental jobs. One example is *The Job Seeker*, available from Rte. 2, Box 16, Warrens, WI 54666. Six issues cost $19.50. A new book, *The Complete Guide to Environmental Careers,* is also available for $14.95 by calling 1-800-828-1302. This book gives an overview of environmental jobs as well as volunteer and internship opportunities.

Besides becoming involved in the organizations, working in an environmental job, or volunteering, you can have a voice in the environmental movement through the political process. Letter writing is an effective means of communicating with our federal officials. The president can be reached by writing to The White House, 1600 Pennsylvania Avenue, NW, Washington, DC 20500. Senators and representatives can be reached by sending letters to the U.S. Senate or U.S. House of Representatives, Washington, DC 20515. Phone calls can also be effective, although you will probably speak only with an aide. The White House switchboard is (202) 456-1414, the U.S. Senate is (202) 224-3121, and the House of Representatives is (202) 456-1414.

It is often beneficial to become politically involved at the local level as well. Usually legislation passed at the state and local levels has more direct impacts on your personal life than does national legislation. It may also be helpful to write to the government agencies administering the policies. A partial list of government agencies, their addresses, and phone numbers is found in the Appendix; a complete list is available at most libraries.

Also increasingly popular in the United States is the Green Party.

Originating in Europe, the Green Party now has representatives in California, New York, Vermont, and Massachusetts, as well as local offices throughout the United States. The Green Organizing committee in the United States can be reached at P.O. Box 40040, St. Paul, MN 55104, or Box 91, Marshfield, VT 05658.

Others would prefer to invest their money rather than or in addition to volunteering actual time. More and more there are companies that make investments only with environmentally oriented companies. There are also credit cards that donate a portion of each credit purchase to a specified environmental organization. A good resource for information on environmental investments is *A Socially Responsible Financing Planning Guide,* available from Co-Op America, 2100 M Street NW, Suite 310, Washington, DC 20036.

Appendix: Government Agencies

Consumer Product Safety Commission
5401 Westbard Avenue
Bethesda, MD 20207
(800) 638–CPSC

Department of Agriculture, U.S. Forest Service
P.O. Box 96090
Washington, DC 20013
(202) 447-2791

Department of Health & Welfare, Food and Drug Administration
5600 Fishers Lane
Rockville, MD 20857
(301) 443-2410

Department of the Interior
18th & C Streets, NW
Washington, DC 20240
  Bureau of Land Management (202) 343-5717
  National Park Service (202) 343-4747
  U.S. Fish & Wildlife Service (202) 343-5634

Environmental Protection Agency
401 M Street, SW
Washington, DC 20460
(202) 382-2080

Federal Energy Regulatory Commission
825 North Capitol Street, NE
Washington, DC 20240
(202) 357-8118

National Oceanic and Atmospheric Administration
14th Street and Constitution Avenue, NW
Washington, DC 20230
(202) 377-8090

Nuclear Regulatory Commission
1717 H Street, NW
Washington, DC 20585
(301) 492-7715

Solar Energy Research Institute
1617 Cole Boulevard
Golden, CO 80401
(303) 231-1000

Suggestions for Further Reading

ALTERNATIVE ENERGY

Alternative Energy Sourcebook 1990: A Comprehensive Catalog of the Finest Low-Voltage Technologies. Ukiah, Calif.: Real Goods Publishers. $10.00.

Beyond Oil. John Gever, Robert Kaufmann, David Skole and Charles Vorosmarty. New York: Ballinger, 1986.

Design for a Limited Planet. Norma Skurka and Jon Naar. New York: Ballantine Books, 1978.

"Energy for Planet Earth." Ged R. Davis. *Scientific American,* September 1990, pp. 55–62.

"Energy from Fossil Fuels." William Fulkerson, Roddie R. Judkins, and Manoj K. Sanghvi. *Scientific American,* September 1990, pp. 129–135.

CHEMICALS, PESTICIDES, TOXIC WASTE

For Our Kids' Sake. Anne Witte Garland. San Francisco: Sierra Club Books, 1989.

Laying Waste: The Poisoning of America by Toxic Chemicals. Michael Brown. New York: Pantheon, 1980.

Silent Spring: 25th Anniversary Edition. Rachel Carson. Boston: Houghton Mifflin, 1987. $8.95.

Zero Discharge: A Citizen's Toxic Waste Manual. Ben Gordon and Peter Montague. Greenpeace, 1989.

CHILDREN'S BOOKS

Animal Rights: Stories of People Who Defend the Rights of Animals. Patricia Curtis. New York: Four Winds, Macmillan Press, 1980. $11.95.

Atlas of Environmental Issues. Nick Middleton. New York: Facts on File, 1989. $16.95.

Chadwick the Crab. Priscilla Cummings. Centreville, Md.: Tidewater Publishers, 1986. $5.95.

Children's Atlas of Wildlife. Edited by Elizabeth Fagan. Chicago: Rand McNally, 1990. $14.95.

Coastal Rescue: Preserving Our Seashores. Christina G. Miller and Louise A. Berry. New York: Atheneum Children's Books/Macmillan, 1989. $12.95.

Coral Reefs. Sylvia A. Johnson. Minneapolis: Lerner Publications, 1984. $12.95.

Handbook of Nature Study. Anna Botsford. San Francisco: Comstock. $26.95.

The Illustrated World of Wild Animals. Mark Carwardine. New York: Simon and Schuster, 1990. $7.95.

The Kids' World Almanac of Animals and Pets. Deborah G. Felder. New York: Pharos Books, 1989. $14.95.

The Lorax. Dr. Seuss. New York: Random House, 1979. $10.95.

Oceans. Martyn Bramwell. New York: Franklin Watts, 1987. $8.49.

Peterson First Guide to Mammals. Peter Alden. Boston: Houghton Mifflin, 1987. $3.95.

The Wump World. Bill Peet. Boston: Houghton Mifflin, 1974. $13.95.

DEFORESTATION/OLD GROWTH FORESTS/ RAIN FORESTS

Ancient Forests of the Pacific Northwest. Elliott A. Norse. Washington, D.C.: Island Press, 1989. $34.95.

The Fate of the Forest: Developers, Destroyers and Defenders of the Amazon. Susanna Hecht and Alexander Cockburn. Washington, D.C.: Island Press, 1989. $24.95.

Forest Primeval: The Natural History of an Ancient Forest. Chris Maser. San Francisco: Sierra Club Books, 1989. $25.00.

Fragile Majesty: The Battle for America's Last Great Forest. Keith Ervin. Seattle: Mountaineers Books, 1989. $14.95.

In the Rainforest. Catherine Caulfield. New York: Alfred A. Knopf, 1984. $24.95.

The Last Rain Forests: A World Conservation Atlas. Edited by Mark Collins. New York: Oxford University Press, 1990. $29.95.

Life Above the Jungle Floor. Donald Perry. New York: Fireside/Simon and Schuster, 1988. $11.95.

Secrets of the Old Growth Forests. David Kelly and Gary Braasch. Layton, Utah: Peregrine Smith, 1990. $15.95.

GARBAGE

The Art of Composting. Metro Service District. (Available from Earth Care Paper, P.O. Box 3335, Madison, WI 53704.)

Here Today, Here Tomorrow. New Jersey Department of Environmental Protection, 1989.

Plastics: America's Packaging Dilemma. Nancy Wolf and Ellen Feldman, Environmental Action Coalition. Washington, D.C.: Island Press, 1990. $19.95.

Rush to Burn: Solving America's Garbage Crisis? From the Editors of Newsday. Washington, D.C.: Island Press, 1989. $14.95.

The Solid Waste Handbook: A Practical Guide. Edited by William D. Robinson. New York: John Wiley, 1986. $94.50.

War on Waste: Can America Win Its Battle with Garbage? Louis Blumberg and Robert Gottlieb. Washington, D.C.: Island Press, 1989. $34.95.

GENERAL ENVIRONMENTAL BOOKS

Beyond the Fray: Reshaping America's Environmental Response. Daniel D. Chiras. Boulder, Colo.: Johnson Books, 1990. $17.95.

Blueprint for a Green Planet. John Seymour and Herbert Girardet. Englewood Cliffs, N.J.: Prentice Hall, 1987. $14.95.

Blueprint for the Environment. A Plan for Federal Action and Advice to President Bush from America's Environmental Community. Edited by T. Allan Comp. Salt Lake City: Howe Brothers, 1989. $13.95.

The Control of Nature. John McPhee. New York: Farrar Straus Giroux, 1989. $17.95.

Crossroads: Environmental Priorities for the Future. Edited by Peter Borrelli. Washington, D.C.: Island Press, 1988. $17.95.

The Crucial Decade: The 1990s and the Global Environmental Challenge. Washington, D.C.: World Resources Institute, 1989. $5.00.

Deep Ecology. Bill Devall and George Sessions. Layton, Utah: Peregrine Smith Books, 1987. $11.95.

The Earth Care Annual 1990. Edited by Russell Wild. National Wildlife Federation. Emmaus, Pa.: Rodale Press, 1990. $17.95.

Ecotopia. Ernest Callenbach. New York: Bantam, 1983. $4.50.

The End of Nature. Bill McKibben. New York: Random House, 1989. $19.95.

Green Justice: The Environment and the Courts. Thomas More Hoban and Richard Oliver Brooks. Boulder: Westview, 1987. $18.95.

In Praise of Nature. Edited by Stephanie Mills. Washington, D.C.: Island Press, 1990. $22.95.

Living in the Environment: An Introduction to Environmental Science. G. Tyler Miller, Jr. Belmont, Calif.: Wadsworth, 1990.

Making Peace with the Planet. Barry Commoner. New York: Pantheon Books, 1990. $19.95.

Nature's End: The Consequences of the Twentieth Century. Whitley Streiber and James Kunetka. New York: Warner Books, 1987. $4.95.

New World, New Mind. Paul Ehrlich and Robert Ornstein. New York: Doubleday, 1989. $18.95.

One Earth, One Future: Our Changing Global Environment. Cheryl Simon Silver, with Ruth S. DeFries for the National Academy of Sciences. Washington, D.C.: National Academy Press, 1990. $14.95.

Small is Beautiful: Economics As If People Mattered. E. F. Schumacher. New York: Harper and Row, 1989. $9.95.

State of the World. Washington, D.C.: Worldwatch Institute, annual. $10.95.

The Wooing of the Earth: New Perspectives on Man's Use of Nature. René Dubos. New York: Charles Scribner's Sons, 1980. $4.95.

The World of Nature. Robin Dunbar. New York: W. H. Smith, 1985. $30.00.

GLOBAL WARMING

The Challenge of Global Warming. Edited by Dean E. Abrahamson. Washington, D.C.: Island Press, 1989. $34.95.

Global Warming. Stephen H. Schmeider. San Francisco: Sierra Club Books, 1989. $18.95.

The Greenhouse Trap: A World Resources Institute Guide to the Environment. Francesca Lyman and the World Resource Institute. Boston: Beacon Press, 1990. $21.95.

The Hole in the Sky. John Gribbon. New York: Bantam, 1988. $4.50.

A Matter of Degrees: The Potential for Controlling the Greenhouse Effect. Irving M. Mintzer and Jonathan Shopley. Washington, D.C.: World Resources Institute, 1987.

Ozone Crisis: The 15-Year Evolution of a Sudden Global Emergency. Sharon L. Roan. New York: John Wiley and Sons, 1989.

The Rising Tide: Global Warming and World Sea Levels. Lynne T. Edgerton. Washington, D.C.: Island Press, 1990. $29.95.

The Sky is the Limit: Strategies for Protecting the Ozone Layer. Irving M. Mintzer. Washington, D.C.: World Resource Institute, 1986.

Turning Down the Heat: Solutions to Global Warming. Public Citizen's Critical Mass Energy Projects, 1988.

INVOLVEMENT IN THE ENVIRONMENT

The Amateur Naturalist. Gerald Durrell with Lee Durrell. New York: Alfred A. Knopf, 1988.

The Complete Guide to Environmental Careers. CEIP Fund. Washington, D.C.: Island Press, 1989. $14.95.

Design for a Livable Planet: How You Can Help Clean Up the Environment. Jon Naar. New York: Harper and Row, 1990.

Ecodefense: A Field Guide to Monkeywrenching. Edited by Dave Foreman and Bill Haywood. Ned Ludd Books, 1987. $12.00.

Ecologue: The Environmental Catalogue and Consumers' Guide for a Safe Earth. Bruce Anderson. Englewood Cliffs, N.J.: Prentice Hall, 1990. $18.95.

Ecotactics: The Sierra Club Handbook for Environmental Activists. Edited by John G. Mitchell with Constance L. Stallings. New York: Simon and Schuster, 1970.

50 Simple Things You Can Do to Save the Earth. The Earth Works Group. Schenevus, N.Y.: Greenleaf, 1989. $4.95.

The Global Ecology Handbook. The Global Tomorrow Coalition. Boston: Beacon Press, 1990. $16.95.

The Green Consumer. John Elkington, Julia Hailes, and Joel Makower. New York: Penguin Books, 1990.

The Green Lifestyles Handbook: 1001 Ways You Can Heal the Earth. Edited by Jeremy Rifkin. New York: Henry Holt & Company, 1990. $10.95.

In Search of Environmental Excellence. Bruce Piasecki and Peter Asmus. New York: Simon and Schuster, 1990. $22.95.

Investing With a Social Conscience. Elizabeth Judd. New York: Pharos Books, 1990. $18.95.

Love Canal: My Story. Lois Marie Gibbs. Albany, N.Y.: State University of New York Press, 1982. $14.95.

The Mail Order Gardener. Hal Morgan. New York: Harper and Row, 1988. $12.95.

The Naturalist's Garden. Ruth Shaw Ernst. Emmaus, Pa.: Rodale Press, 1987. $19.95.

Nature with Children of all Ages. Edith A. Sisson. Englewood Cliffs, N.J.: Prentice Hall Press, 1982. $12.95.

The New Organic Grower. Eliot Coleman. Post Mills, Vt.: Chelsea Green Publishers, 1989. $19.95.

NOT in Our Backyards! Community Action for Health and the Environment. Nicholas Freudenberg. New York: Monthly Review Press, 1984. $10.00.

Organizing: A Guide for Grassroots Leaders. Si Kahn. New York: McGraw-Hill, 1981. $7.95.

Restoring the Earth: How Americans Are Working to Renew Our Damaged Environment. John J. Berger. New York: Alfred A. Knopf, 1985. $18.95.

Save Our Planet: 750 Everyday Ways You Can Help Clean Up the Earth. Diane MacEachern. New York: Dell Publishers, 1990. $9.95.

Saving the Earth: A Citizen's Guide to Environmental Action. Will Steger and Jon Bowermaster. New York: Alfred A. Knopf, 1990. $24.95.

Simple in Means, Rich in Ends: Practicing Deep Ecology. Bill Devall. Layton Utah: Peregrine Smith, 1988. $12.95.

MAGAZINES/ PERIODICALS/ NEWSPAPERS

BioCycle: Journal of Waste Recycling. P.O. Box 351, Emmaus, PA 18049. (215) 967–4135. $44.00 per year for 12 issues.

Buzzworm: The Environmental Journal. 1818 16th Street, Boulder, CO 80302. (303) 442–1969. $18.00 per year for 6 issues.

E Magazine. P.O. Box 5098, Westport, CT 06881. (203) 854–5559. $20 per year for 6 issues.

Environment. Heldreff Publications, 4000 Albemarle Street,

NW, Washington, DC 20016. (202) 362–6445. $23.00 per year for 10 issues.

EPA Journal. Superintendent of Documents, Government Printing Office, Washington, DC 20402. (202) 362–6445. $8.00 per year for 6 issues.

Garbage: The Practical Journal for the Environment. 435 Ninth Street, Brooklyn, NY 11215. (800) 274–9909. $21.00 per year for 6 issues.

Green Magazine for Our Environment. 5 Riverside Park Industrial Area, Billet Lane, Berkhampsted, Herts HP4 1BR, United Kingdom. £42.95 per year for 13 issues sent to the United States.

Harrowsmith. Ferry Road, Charlotte, VT 05445 (802) 425–3961. $24.00 per year for 6 issues.

High Country News. High Country Foundation, Box 1090, Paonia, CO 81428. (303) 527-4898. $24.00 per year, published biweekly.

The WorldPaper. 20 World Trade Center, Boston, MA 02210. (617) 439-5400.

ORGANIZATIONS

Cousteau: The Captain and His World. Richard Munson. Edited by Bruce Lee. New York: William Morrow, 1989. $19.95.

The History of the Sierra Club: 1892-1970. Michael P. Cohen. San Francisco: Sierra Club Books, 1988. $29.95.

Love Canal: A Chronology of Events that Shaped a Movement. Citizen's Clearinghouse for Hazardous Wate, n.d.

Wild by Law: The Sierra Club Legal Defense Fund and the Places It Has Saved. Tom Turner. San Francisco: Sierra Club Books, 1990. $50.00.

POLLUTION/ACID RAIN

Acid Rain Information Book. David V. Bubenick. Park Ridge, N.J.: Noyes, 1984. $39.00.

The Healthy Home: An Attic to Basement Guide to Toxin-Free Living. Linda Mason Hunter. Emmaus, Pa.: Rodale Press, 1989. $21.95.

The Toxic Cloud: The Poisoning of America's Air. Michael H. Brown. New York: Harper and Row, 1988. $9.95.

POPULATION

The Population Explosion. Paul R. Ehrlich and Anne H. Ehrlich. New York: Simon and Schuster, 1990. $18.95.

WATER RESOURCES/OCEANS

A Citizen's Guide to Plastics in the Ocean. Kathryn J. O'Hara and Suzanne Iudicello. Washington, D.C.: Center for Marine Conservation, 1988. $2.00.

The Edge of the Sea. Rachel Carson. Boston: Houghton Mifflin, 1979. $9.95.

In the Wake of the "Exxon Valdez": The Devastating Impact of the Alaska Oil Spill. Art Davidson. San Francisco: Sierra Club Books, 1990. $18.95.

The Living Ocean: Understanding and Protecting Marine Biodiversity. Boyd Thorne-Miller and John Catena. Washington, D.C.: Island Press, 1990. $10.95.

Rivers at Risk: The Concerned Citizen's Guide to Hydropower. John D. Echeverria, Pope Barrow, and Richard Roos-Collins. Washington, D.C.: Island Press, 1989. $29.95.

The Sea Around Us. Rachel L. Carson. New York: Oxford University Press, 1989. $18.95.

Voyage to the Whales. Hal Whitehead. Post Mills, Vt.: Chelsea Green Publishers, 1990. $22.50.

The Wasted Ocean. David K. Bulloch. New York: Lyons and Burford, 1989. $9.95.

Western Water Made Simple. By the Editors of *High Country News.* Washington, D.C.: Island Press, 1987. $15.95.

WILDERNESS AND NATURAL AREAS

The Exploration of the Colorado River and Its Canyons. John Wesley Powell. New York: Penguin, 1987. $6.95.

Marine Parks and Aquaria of the United States. Anthony L. Pacheco and Susan E. Smith. New York: Lyons & Burford, 1990. $16.95.

The Mountains of California. John Muir. Golden, Colo.: Fulcrum, 1988. $22.95.

Our National Wetland Heritage: A Protection Guidebook. John A. Kusler. Washington, D.C.: Environmental Law Institute, 1983. $14.00.

Redouté's Fairest Flowers. Martyn Rix and William T. Stearn. Englewood Cliffs, N.J.: Prentice Hall Press, 1987. $35.00.

Vanishing Arctic: Alaska's National Wildlife Refuge. T.H. Watkins. New York: Aperture, 1988. $29.95.

Washington's Wild Rivers: The Unfinished Work. Tim McNulty. Seattle: The Mountaineers Books, 1990. $35.00.

Wetlands: Mitigating and Regulating Development Impacts. David Salvesen. Washington, D.C.: Island Press, 1990. $38.00.

Wildflowers of the American West. Rose Houk. San Francisco: Chronicle Books, 1987. $14.95.

Yellowstone's Red Summer. Alen Carey and Sandy Carey. Flagstaff, Ariz: Northland Press, 1989. $19.95.

WILDLIFE AND DOMESTIC ANIMALS

The Endangered Kingdom: The Struggle to Save America's Wildlife. Roger DiSilvestro. New York: John Wiley and Sons, 1989. $19.95.

The Practical Ornithologist. John Gooders. New York: Simon and Schuster, 1990. $24.95.

Seasons of the Seal. Fred Bruemmer and Brian Davies. Minocqua, Wis.: Northword, 1988. $34.95.

The Survival Factor. Mike and Tim Birkhead. New York: Facts on File, 1990. $24.95.

Wild America. Jayne Loader. New York: Ivy Books, 1990. $4.95.

Wildlife in Peril: The Endangered Mammals of Colorado. John A. Murray. Niwot, Colo.: Roberts Rinehart, 1987. $10.95.

Index